WORSHIP & SONG

Pew Edition

Abingdon Press
Nashville

INTRODUCTION

Worship in the Christian church in the United States, once quite homogenous, is becoming increasingly diverse. Some local churches offer different styles of worship in different services. Others focus exclusively on one style. Still others incorporate elements of several styles in the same service. And congregational worship music reflects that diversity of worship style and practice.

Worship & Song has been compiled to supplement hymnals and songbooks currently in use, particularly *The United Methodist Hymnal* (1989) and *The Faith We Sing* (2000). There are no duplications of content between *Worship & Song* and either of its predecessors. The music is intended to be representative of the breadth of current worship practice, providing new material in several musical genres and including older material not appearing in former United Methodist collections. It also provides music from many different styles to churches that offer primarily one worship style who desire to broaden their repertoire. Praise music, recently written hymns, gospel songs, world music, music from various ethnic traditions, music from the Taizé and Iona communities, and various pieces of service music are all included.

The Pew Edition is intended for congregational use; songs intended to be sung in unison (or in parts) are printed in unison (or in parts). The Accompaniment Edition is for keyboard players, with some songs given both stylistic and simplified versions; it also includes basic chord symbols for guitarists. The Singer's Edition is intended for choirs and includes some choral harmonizations, descants, and endings. The Leader's Edition is a photographic enlargement of the Pew Edition allowing leaders to see it from a podium; it also includes descriptions of each song and several additional indexes. The Worship Resources Edition contains no music but rather over 200 prayers, litanies, affirmations, and other acts of worship. The Presentation Edition includes the words of all songs and worship resources on electronic files suitable for projection. An Internet Edition will include online versions of the majority of the books' contents for downloading. It will also allow for the continual addition of new songs and prayers even after original publication.

Worship hymns and songs and prayers are constantly being written and used. The publication of *Worship & Song* creates a snapshot of the rich variety of resources available to the church. It is my prayer that the print, digital, and Internet editions of *Worship & Song*, along with those future materials still to be published, will enrich your faith journey.

Gary Alan Smith
General Editor and Project Director

Pew Edition   ISBN 978-1-42670-993-7 (Emblem)   Worship Resources Edition   ISBN 978-1-42670-997-5
Pew Edition   ISBN 978-1-42672-552-4 (Non-Emblem)   Presentation Edition   UPC 843504009809
Leader's Edition   ISBN 978-1-42670-994-4   Pew Edition Sampler   UPC 843504020439
Singer's Edition   ISBN 978-1-42670-995-1   Accompaniment Edition Sampler   UPC 843504020446
Accompaniment Edition   ISBN 978-1-42670-996-8

14 15 16 17 18 19 20 — 10 9 8 7 6 5

MANUFACTURED IN THE UNITED STATES OF AMERICA

O For a Thousand Tongues to Sing   3001

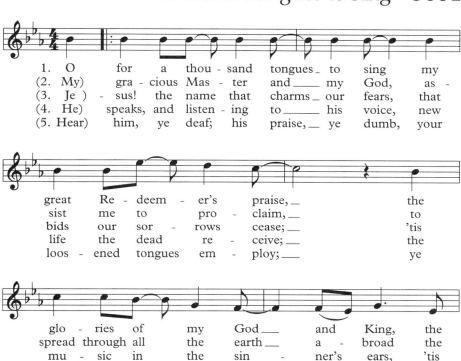

1. O   for   a   thou - sand tongues _ to   sing   my
(2. My)   gra - cious Mas - ter   and ____ my   God,   as -
(3. Je) - sus! the name that   charms _ our   fears, that
(4. He)   speaks, and listen - ing to _____ his   voice, new
(5. Hear) him, ye   deaf; his   praise, _ ye   dumb, your

great   Re - deem - er's   praise, _   the
sist   me   to   pro - claim, _   to
bids   our sor - rows   cease; _   'tis
life   the dead   re - ceive; _   the
loos - ened tongues em - ploy; _   ye

glo - ries   of   my   God ___   and   King,   the
spread through all the   earth ___ a - broad   the
mu - sic   in   the   sin -   ner's ears,   'tis
mourn - ful, bro - ken hearts _ re - joice,   the
blind, be - hold your Sav -   ior   come,   and

tri - umphs of   his grace, _ the tri - umphs of his grace! _
hon - ors of   thy name, _ the hon - ors of   thy name. _
life, and health, and peace, _ 'tis life, and health, and peace. _
hum - ble poor be - lieve, _ the hum - ble poor be - lieve. _
leap, ye   lame, for joy, ___ and leap, ye lame, for joy, ___

| 1-4 | | 5 |

___   2. My
___   3. Je -
___   4. He
___   5. Hear

                for   joy! _____

WORDS: Charles Wesley
MUSIC: Mark A. Miller

Music © 2000 Abingdon Press, admin. by The Copyright Company

AZMON'S GHOST
CM

3002 Blessed Be Your Name

1. Bless - ed be your name in the
2. Bless - ed be your name when the

land that is plen - ti - ful, where your
sun's shin - ing down on me, when the

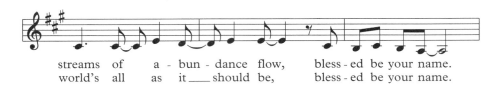

streams of a - bun - dance flow, bless - ed be your name.
world's all as it should be, bless - ed be your name.

Bless - ed be your name when I'm
Bless - ed be your name on the

found in the des - ert place, though I
road marked with suf - fer - ing, though there's

walk through the wil - der - ness, bless - ed be your name.
pain in the of - fer - ing, bless - ed be your name.

Ev - ery bless - ing you pour out I'll

WORDS: Matt Redman and Beth Redman
MUSIC: Matt Redman and Beth Redman

BLESSED BE YOUR NAME
Irr. with Refrain

3003 How Great Is Our God

1. The splen-dor of the King, __ __ clothed in maj - es-ty; ____
2. Age to age he stands, _ and time is in his hands; _

__ let all the earth re - joice, _ let all the earth re - joice. _
__ Be - gin-ning and the End, _ Be - gin-ning and the End. _

__ He wraps _ him - self in light, _ and
__ The God - head, Three - in - one, __ __

dark - ness tries to hide; __ it trem-bles at his voice, __
Fa - ther, Spir - it, Son, __ the Li - on and the Lamb, _

Refrain

__ it trem-bles at his voice. __ How great _
__ the Li - on and the Lamb. _

__ is our God! _ Sing with me, "How great is our God!" _

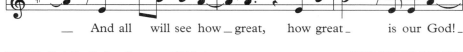

__ And all will see how _ great, how great _ is our God! _

WORDS: Chris Tomlin, Jesse Reeves, and Ed Cash
MUSIC: Chris Tomlin, Jesse Reeves, and Ed Cash

HOW GREAT IS OUR GOD
Irr. with Refrain

Step by Step

3004

Name a-bove all names, wor-thy of all praise; my

heart will sing, "How great _ is our God!" _

O God, you are my God, and I will ev-er praise

you. O God, you are my God, and I will ev-er praise

you. I will seek you in the morn - ing, and I will

learn to walk in your ways; and step by step you'll lead _

_ me, and I will fol-low you all of my days.

WORDS: David Strasser
MUSIC: David Strasser

STEP BY STEP
Irr.

3005 Fill Us with Your Love, O Lord

Refrain
Leader (or All)

Fill us with your love, __ O Lord, and

we will sing for joy. _____ Fill us with your love, _

_ O Lord, and we will sing for joy. __

All

Fill us with your love, __ O Lord, and

we will sing for joy. _____ Fill us with your love, _

WORDS: Carol Browning (Ps. 90:12-17)　　　　　　　　　　　　　　　　FILL US
MUSIC: Carol Browning　　　　　　　　　　　　　　　　　　　　Irr. with Refrain

Last time to Coda

_ O Lord, and we will sing for joy. _

1 Leader (or All)

Teach us to num - ber our days _ a - right that we may have wis - dom of heart. _ Re - turn, O Lord! How long? Have pit - y on your ser - vants.

2 Leader (or All)

Fill us at day - break with _ your kind - ness; we will sing for joy all our days. _ Make us as glad as of old we were sad, in the years when we saw e - vil.

Alleluia

Al - le - lu - ia! Al - le - lu - ia!

Al - le - lu - ia! Al - le - lu - ia!

WORDS: Traditional liturgical text
MUSIC: Norah Duncan IV

ALLELUIA (DUNCAN)
44.44

Laudate Dominum
(Sing, Praise and Bless the Lord)

Latin Lau - da - te Do - mi - num, lau - da - te Do - mi - num,
English Sing, praise and bless the Lord. Sing, praise and bless the Lord.

om - nes gen - tes, Al - le - lu - ia! Al - le - lu - ia!
Peo - ples! Na - tions! Al - le - lu - ia! Al - le - lu - ia!

WORDS: The Community of Taizé
MUSIC: Jacques Berthier

LAUDATE DOMINUM
66.44

3008 Open the Eyes of My Heart

O - pen the eyes of my heart, — Lord,

o-pen the eyes of my heart; — I want to see you,

I want to see you. O-pen the eyes of my heart, —

— Lord, o-pen the eyes of my heart; — I want to

see you, I want to see you. To see you

high and lift - ed up, — shin-ing in the light of your glo-

ry. Pour out your pow - er and love —

Third time to Coda

— as we sing. Ho - ly, ho - ly, ho -

| 1 | 2 | *D.S. al Coda* |

ly. ly. To see you

WORDS: Paul Baloche
MUSIC: Paul Baloche

EYES OF MY HEART
Irr.

⊕ CODA

(optional a cappella repeat)

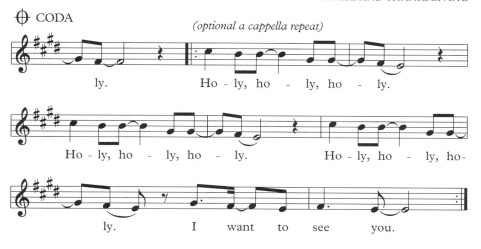

ly.

Ho - ly, ho - ly, ho - ly.

Ho - ly, ho - ly, ho - ly.

Ho - ly, ho - ly, ho-

ly.   I   want   to   see   you.

Praise God for This Holy Ground   3009

1. Praise God   for   this   ho - ly ground,
2. Praise God   in   whose word we   find
3. Praise God   who   through Christ makes known
4. Praise God's Spir - it   who   be - friends,
5. Though praise ends, praise is   be - gun

place   and   peo - ple,   sight   and   sound.
food   for   bod - y,   soul,   and   mind.
all   are   loved   and   called God's own.
rais - es,   hum - bles,   breaks,   and   mends.
where   God's will   is   glad - ly   done.

Refrain

Hal - le - lu - jah! Hal - le - lu - jah! Hal - le - lu - jah! God's

good - ness   is   e - ter - nal.

WORDS: John L. Bell
MUSIC: John L. Bell

HEYMONYSTRAAT
77 with Refrain

© 2002 WGRG, Iona Community (Scotland), admin. by GIA Publications, Inc.

3010 Sing of the Lord's Goodness

1. Sing of the Lord's good-ness, Fa-ther of all wis-dom,
2. Pow-er he has wield-ed, hon-or is his gar-ment,
3. Cour-age in our dark-ness, com-fort in our sor-row,
4. Praise him with your sing-ing, praise him with the trum-pet,

come to him and bless his name. Mer-cy he has shown us,
ris-en from the snares of death. His word he has spo-ken,
Spir-it of our God most high; sol-ace for the wea-ry,
praise God with the lute and harp; praise him with the cym-bals,

his love is for-ev-er, faith-ful to the end of days.
one bread he has brok-en, new life he now gives to all.
par-don for the sin-ner, splen-dor of the liv-ing God.
praise him with your danc-ing, praise God till the end of days.

Refrain

Come then, all you na-tions, sing of your Lord's good-ness,

me-lo-dies of praise and thanks to God.

Ring out the Lord's glo-ry, praise him with your mu-sic,

wor-ship him and bless his name.

WORDS: Ernest Sands
MUSIC: Ernest Sands

THE LORD'S GOODNESS
12 7.12 7 with Refrain

All My Days

3011

1. You know my words be - fore they're said. You
2. If I should fly be - yond the dawn, the
3. Our ev - ery thought, each word we say, the
4. O mend my heart and free my voice. From

know my need and I am fed. You
dark - ness will not o - ver - come. If
whole of time, the pres - ent day, are
sin re - leased, I will re - joice. O

give me life. You know my ways, my
I lie down in deep - est night, still
held with - in your might - y hand, too
search me, Lord, my spir - it cries, and

strength, my path, for all my days, my
you are there, my Lord, my light, still
won - der - ful to com - pre - hend, too
let my song of praise a - rise, and

1-3

strength, my path, for all my days. ___
you are there, my Lord, my light. ___
won - der - ful to com - pre - hend! ___
let my song of

4

praise a - rise! ___

WORDS: Laurie Zelman
MUSIC: Mark A. Miller

HIXON
88.88

3012 When Words Alone Cannot Express

Unison

1. When words a - lone can - not ex - press
2. When speech e - rodes and tem - pers flare,
3. When bread is bro - ken, wine is poured,
4. With - in each sea - son of our lives,

all that our hearts ache to con - fess,
when peace gives way to i - dle dare,
when we en - coun - ter Christ the Lord,
when ev - ery pas - sage - way ar - rives,

Harmony

bring mu - sic! Al - le - lu - ia!
bring mu - sic! Al - le - lu - ia!
bring mu - sic! Al - le - lu - ia!
bring mu - sic! Al - le - lu - ia!

Unison

Bring mel - o - dy and rhyth - mic fire!
Let psalms re - store our mem - o - ry
When chil - dren teach us how to pray,
Sing when the in - fant draws a breath;

Bring in - stru - ments, bring bells and choir!
that God has made us to be free!
when sim - ple he - roes show the way,
sing when the el - der yields to death.

WORDS: John Thornburg
MUSIC: *Geistliche Kirchengesänge*, 1623

LASST UNS ERFREUEN
88.34.88 with Refrain

Harmony

Bring mu - sic! Al - le - lu - ia! Al - le - lu - ia!
Bring mu - sic! Al - le - lu - ia! Al - le - lu - ia!
bring mu - sic! Al - le - lu - ia! Al - le - lu - ia!
Bring mu - sic! Al - le - lu - ia! Al - le - lu - ia!

Unison

Al - le - lu - ia! Al - le - lu - ia!
Al - le - lu - ia! Al - le - lu - ia!
Al - le - lu - ia! Al - le - lu - ia!
Al - le - lu - ia! Al - le - lu - ia!

Sing the Praise of God Our Maker   3013

1. Sing the praise of God our Mak - er, source of won - der,
2. Sing the praise of Christ our Broth - er, sage whose words speak
3. Sing the praise of Ho - ly Spir - it, spark in hu - man

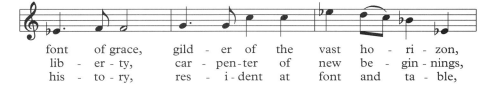

font of grace, gild - er of the vast ho - ri - zon,
lib - er - ty, car - pen - ter of new be - gin - nings,
his - to - ry, res - i - dent at font and ta - ble,

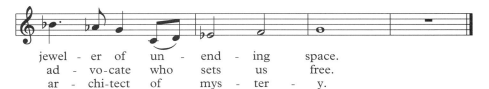

jewel - er of un - end - ing space.
ad - vo - cate who sets us free.
ar - chi - tect of mys - ter - y.

WORDS: John Thornburg
MUSIC: Sally Ann Morris

© 2008 GIA Publications, Inc.

BROTHER
87.87

3014   You Are Good

Lord, you are good, and your mer-cy en-dur-eth for-ev - er. Lord, you are good, and your mer-cy en-dur-eth for-ev - er.

Peo - ple from ev-e - ry na - tion and tongue, from gen-er-a-tion to gen-er - a - tion:

Refrain

we wor-ship you, __ Hal - le - lu - jah! Hal-le-lu - jah! We wor-ship you __ for who you are! __

We wor - ship you, __

Last time to Coda

Hal-le-lu - jah! Hal - le-lu - jah! We

WORDS: Israel Houghton
MUSIC: Israel Houghton

YOU ARE GOOD
Irr.

3015 How Great You Are

1. How great __ you are! __ How won - der - ful your
(2. How great) __ you are! __ How awe-some, Lord, your

ways, O God. So sings my soul, my Sav -
might - y hand. The sun, the moon and stars __

ior, God, to thee. __ How great __ you are! __
__ you hold in place. __ How great __ you are! __

__ Be - fore the world you knew my name. You
__ Your bound-less love has filled my life. I

formed me, Lord, to wor - ship at your feet. _____
live now in the pow - er of your grace. _____

Refrain

How great __ you are! __ How beau - ti - ful the

glo - ry of my King! How great __ you are! __

How great __ you are! __

WORDS: Phil Posthuma
MUSIC: Phil Posthuma
© 2006 Phil Posthuma

POSTHUMA
4 8 10 D with Refrain

3016   What a Mighty God We Serve

What a might - y God we serve.

What a might - y God we serve.

An-gels bow be - fore you, heaven and earth a - dore you.

What a might - y God we serve.

WORDS: Traditional African folk song
MUSIC: Traditional African folk song; arr. by Jackson Henry

Arr. © 2011 Jackson Henry

MIGHTY GOD
Irr.

Come, Join the Dance of Trinity 3017

1. Come, join the dance of Trin - i - ty, be - fore all worlds be - gun — the in - ter - weav - ing of the Three: the Fa - ther, Spir - it, Son. The u - ni - verse of space and time did not a - rise by chance, but as the Three in love and hope, made room with - in their dance.

2. Come, see the face of Trin - i - ty, new - born in Beth - le - hem; then blood - ied by a crown of thorns out - side Je - ru - sa - lem. The dance of Trin - i - ty is meant for hu - man flesh and bone; when fear con - fines the dance in death, God rolls a - way the stone.

3. Come, speak a - loud of Trin - i - ty, as wind and tongues of flame set peo - ple free at Pen - te - cost to tell the Sav - ior's name. We know the yoke of sin and death, our necks have worn it smooth; go tell the world of weight and woe that we are free to move!

4. With - in the dance of Trin - i - ty, be - fore all worlds be - gun, we sing the prais - es of the Three: the Fa - ther, Spir - it, Son. Let voic - es rise and in - ter - weave, by love and hope set free, to shape in song this joy, this life: the dance of Trin - i - ty.

WORDS: Richard Leach
MUSIC: Traditional English melody

KINGSFOLD
CMD

Words © 2001 Selah Publishing Co., Inc.

3018

Creation Sings

1. Cre - a - tion sings! And we are in the mu - sic, the move-ment of God's en - er - gy and art, a lit - ur - gy that links our life to an - gels, a lit - a - ny that ris - es from the

2. Cre - a - tion groans at our dis - cor - dant clash - ing: the Spir - it comes with mu - sic as our friend to bring the har - mo - ny of peace and beau - ty, to teach the tex - tures of the way to

WORDS: Shirley Erena Murray
MUSIC: Traditional Irish melody; transcription by Dean McIntyre

LONDONDERRY AIR
Irr.

heart. The Spir - it sings! Through love and lam - en -
blend. O God, you draw the mel - o - dy from

ta - tion, from Pen - te - cost to joy of Eas - ter
si - lence, you make of us the in - stru-ments of

Day the u - ni - verse is res - o - nant with
song! We of - fer thanks in wor - ship and in

mu - sic, the small-est crea - ture danc-es to its play.
won - der that such a gift to hu-man souls be - long.

3019 Bidden, Unbidden

1. Wheth-er I cry out your name, or I feel all a-lone, a-
2. If I don't feel you a-round, there is no pic-ture and no

shamed, you are not gone, you are there! _____ Wheth-er I
sound, I will be-lieve you are there! _____ E-ven on

no-tice your hand, in all the stars, the sea, the
my dark-est days I will still sing a word of

land, wheth-er or not, you are there! _____
praise. I will be-lieve you are there! _____

Refrain

Bid-den, un-bid-den, I know you are there. You are pres-ent

al-ways, a-gain and a-gain. _____

If I for-get you, or join you in

prayer, you are pres-ent al-ways for-ev-er. A-men. _____

WORDS: Jenni Lee Boyden and Rusty Edwards
MUSIC: Rusty Edwards

JEWEL
787 D with Refrain

God of the Bible

1. God of the Bi - ble, God in the Gos - pel,
2. God in our strug - gles, God in our hun - ger,
3. Those with - out sta - tus, those who are noth - ing,
4. Not by your fin - ger, not by your an - ger
5. Hope we must car - ry, shin - ing and cer - tain

hope seen in Je - sus, hope yet to come,
suf - fer - ing with us, tak - ing our part,
you have made roy - al, gift - ed with rights,
will our world or - der change in a day,
through all our tur - moil, ter - ror, and loss,

you are our cen - ter, day - light or dark - ness,
still you em - power us, moth - er - ing Spir - it,
cho - sen as part - ners, mid - wives of jus - tice,
but by your peo - ple, fear - less and faith - ful,
bond - ing us glad - ly one to the oth - er,

free - dom or pris - on, you are our home.
feed - ing, sus - tain - ing, from your own heart.
birth - ing new sys - tems, light - ing new lights.
small pa - per lan - terns, light - ing the way.
till our world chang - es fac - ing the cross.

Refrain

Fresh as the morn - ing, sure as the sun - rise, God al-ways faith-ful,

you do not change. Fresh as the morn - ing, sure as the sun - rise,

Last time

God al-ways faith-ful, you do not change.

WORDS: Shirley Erena Murray
MUSIC: Tony E. Alonso

FRESH AS THE MORNING
55.54 D with Refrain

3021 Everlasting God

Strength will rise as we wait upon the Lord, we will wait upon the Lord, we will wait upon the Lord.

Strength will rise as we wait upon the Lord, we will wait upon the Lord, we will wait upon the Lord. Our God, you reign forever, our Hope, our strong Deliverer.

Refrain

You are the everlasting God, the everlasting God. You do not faint, you won't grow weary.

WORDS: Brenton Brown and Ken Riley
MUSIC: Brenton Brown and Ken Riley

EVERLASTING GOD
Irr.

You're the de - fend - er of the weak; _ you com-

fort those in need; _ you lift ___ us up on

wings like ea - gles. _____

Peace of Our Praying 3022

1. Peace of our pray - ing, Song of our sing - ing,
2. Peace of our pray - ing, Christ of our cry - ing,
3. Peace of our pray - ing, Faith of for - giv - ing,

Truth of our tell - ing, Love of all loves,
Strength of our striv - ing, Heart of our heart,
Way of our walk - ing, King of all kings,

Health of our heal - ing, Gift of our giv - ing,
Bread of our break - ing, Wine of our wait - ing,
Breath of our breath - ing, Cour - age of car - ing,

Life of our liv - ing, Light of all lights.
Blood of our boast - ing, Death of all death.
Hope of our hop - ing, Life of all life.

WORDS: Terry W. York
MUSIC: C. David Bolin

PAHOA
55.54 D

3023

Forever

1. Give thanks to the Lord, our
(2.) might - y hand and
From the ris - ing to the

God and King; his love en - dures for - ev -
out - stretched arm, his love en - dures for - ev -
set - ting sun, his love en - dures for - ev -

er. For he is good, he is a -
er. For the life that's
er. And by the grace of God we will

bove all things; his love en - dures for - ev - er.
been re - born; his love en - dures for - ev - er.
car - ry on; his love en - dures for - ev - er. } Sing

1.
praise, _____ sing _ praise! _____ 2. With a _ praise! _

2, 3

Refrain

_ Sing praise, _____ sing _ praise! _____ For - ev -

er God is faith - ful, for - ev - er God is strong, _

Last time to Coda

_ for - ev - er God is with _ us, for - ev -

WORDS: Chris Tomlin
MUSIC: Chris Tomlin

FOREVER
Irr.

D.S. al Coda

2

er, for-ev - er! _____

CODA

er, for - ev - er! _____

With You, O Lord

3024

With you, O Lord, is life in all its full - ness, and

in your light we shall see true light.

With you, O Lord, is life in all its full - ness, and

in your light we shall see true light.

WORDS: Community of Taizé (Ps. 36:10)
MUSIC: Jacques Berthier

WITH YOU
11 9.11 9

3025   God Is Speaking

1. God is speak-ing. God is speak-ing. Do you hear?
2. God is speak-ing, al - ways speak-ing us - ing needs,
3. God is speak-ing. God is speak-ing. Do you hear,

Do you hear? Trust and you will hear him.
us - ing joys, speak-ing in his wis - dom,
hear his heart? Trust and you will hear him

Trust and you will hear him. God is love. God is love.
speak-ing in his mer - cy, call - ing hearts, chang-ing lives.
if you want to hear him. God is love, al - ways love.

WORDS: Ken Bible
MUSIC: Traditional French melody

FRÈRE JACQUES
44.33.66.33

3026   God Is Good, All the Time

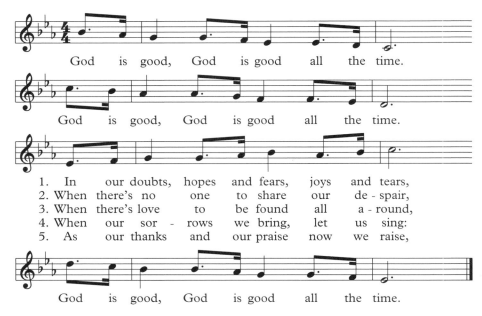

God is good, God is good all the time.

God is good, God is good all the time.

1. In our doubts, hopes and fears, joys and tears,
2. When there's no one to share our de - spair,
3. When there's love to be found all a - round,
4. When our sor - rows we bring, let us sing:
5. As our thanks and our praise now we raise,

God is good, God is good all the time.

WORDS: Dean McIntyre
MUSIC: Dean McIntyre

GOD IS GOOD
99.99

Hallelujah

1., 3. Your love is a - maz - ing, stead-y and un - chang-
(2. Your love is sur - pris) - ing, I can feel it ris -

ing. Your love is a moun - tain, firm be - neath my feet. _
ing, all the joy that's grow - ing deep in - side of me. _

_ Your love is a mys - tery, how you gent - ly lift _
_ Ev - ery time I see _ you all your good-ness shines _

_ me. When I am sur - round - ed your love car - ries me. _
_ through. I can feel this God _ song ris - ing up in me. _

Refrain

Hal - le - lu - jah! Hal - le - lu -

WORDS: Brenton Brown and Brian Doerksen
MUSIC: Brenton Brown and Brian Doerksen

YOUR LOVE IS AMAZING
Irr. with Refrain

3028

Holy Is the Lord

We stand and lift up our hands, _ for the joy _ of the Lord is our strength. _ We bow down and wor- ship him now; how great, _ how awe - some is he! _ And to-geth - er we sing: ___

Refrain

Ho - ly is the Lord _ God Al - might- y, the earth _ is filled with his glo - ry. Ho - ly is the Lord _ God Al - might-

WORDS: Chris Tomlin and Louie Giglio
MUSIC: Chris Tomlin and Louie Giglio

GIGLIO
Irr. with Refrain

3029 In the Desert, on God's Mountain

1. In the des - ert, on God's moun - tain, Mo - ses saw the
2. On Mount Hor - eb Mo - ses halt - ed, stood un - shod on
3. "I AM THAT I AM has called you," spoke the in - can -
4. Mo - ses hid his face in ter - ror, of - fered his ob -
5. La - ter in the wild of Si - nai, from an - oth - er
6. Far from des - erts, far from moun - tains, yearns a bound hu -

bush a - flame, won-dered at the fi - ery fo - liage,
ho - ly ground, felt the puls - ing of God's pres - ence,
des - cent voice. Mo - ses felt the mes - sage sear - ing
jec - tions four: doubt of worth and doubt of tal - ent,
moun - tain height, bring - ing prom - ise to his peo - ple,
man - i - ty. Filled with fire of ho - ly ground-ing,

heard the crack - ling call his name. May we no - tice
sensed the ho - li - ness a - round. May we stop a -
to the heart of will and choice. May we pause to
lack of trust and lack of lore. May we set a -
Mo - ses shone with God's own light. May we, not con -
burn - ing bush - es may we be, draw - ing all to

WORDS: Susan Palo Cherwien
MUSIC: John Goss

LAUDA ANIMA
87.87.87

bush - es burn - ing; may we won - der at the flame.
mid life's la - bor; may we hon - or ho - ly ground.
an - swer sum-mons; may we hear God's burn - ing voice.
side ex - cus - es; may we take the task be - fore.
sumed, yet burn - ing, guide all to the moun-tain height.
God's bright pres - ence — bea-cons of di - vin - i - ty.

Eternal God Transcending Time 3030

1. E - ter - nal God tran-scend - ing time, yet mind - ful of the
2. In - car - nate God re - vealed in time, true Word in flesh re -
3. Life-breath-ing God en - liv - ening time, a - wak - ing heart and
4. Great Tri - une God, so bless the time en - trust - ed to our

fears, the hopes, the ques - tions raised for us by
told, who marked the years from birth to death, then
tongue, in - spir - ing proph - ets, bring - ing hope, con -
care, that all our var - ied min - is - tries may

ev - er-chang - ing years: so guide us through our
rose to break death's hold: by your be - com - ing
sol - ing old and young: draw us to those de -
form a com - mon prayer; then when time ceas - es,

pil - grim days that we may find a home where
one with us, help us to know and claim the
nied your gifts by bi - as, want, or strife, con -
bring us where di - vi - sions are un - done, that

jus - tice, truth, and mer - cy meet, ful - filled in your sha - lom.
u - ni - ty of all bap - tized in your re-deem - ing name.
vert our wills and form through us new chan-nels of your life.
in your pres - ence, joined in praise, at last we may be one.

WORDS: Carl P. Daw, Jr.
MUSIC: USA folk melody, Walker's *Southern Harmony*
Words © 1999 Hope Publishing Company

RESIGNATION
CMD

3031 God Leads Us Along

1. In shad - y, green pas - tures, so rich and so sweet,
2. Some - times on the mount where the sun shines so bright,
3. Though sor - rows be - fall us and e - vils op - pose,

God leads his dear chil - dren a - long;
God leads his dear chil - dren a - long;
God leads his dear chil - dren a - long;

where the wa - ter's cool flow bathes the wea - ry one's feet,
some - times in the val - ley, in dark - est of night,
through grace we can con - quer, de - feat all our foes,

God leads his dear chil - dren a - long.
God leads his dear chil - dren a - long.
God leads his dear chil - dren a - long.

WORDS: G. A. Young
MUSIC: G. A. Young

GOD LEADS US
Irr. with Refrain

Refrain

Some through the wa - ters, some through the flood,

some through the fire, but all through the blood;

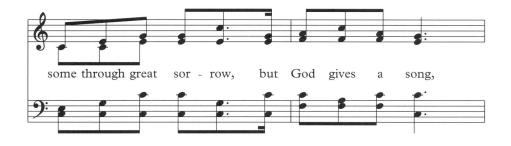

some through great sor - row, but God gives a song,

in the night sea - son and all the day long.

3032

Across the Lands

1. You're the   Word   of God   the   Fa - ther   from be -
(2. Yet you)   left   the gaze   of   an - gels,   came to
(3. With a)   shout   you rose   vic - to - rious,   wrest - ing

fore   the world   be -   gan;   ev - ery   star   and ev - ery
seek   and save   the   lost   and ex - changed the joy   of
vic - tory from   the   grave   and as - cend - ed   in - to

plan - et   has been fash - ioned by   your hand.   All cre -
heav - en   for the   an - guish of   a   cross.   With a
heav - en,   lead - ing cap - tives in   your way.   Now you

a - tion holds   to - geth - er   by the pow - er   of your
prayer you fed   the hun - gry,   with a word you calmed the
stand be - fore   the Fa - ther,   in - ter - ced - ing for your

voice.   Let the skies   de - clare your glo - ry;   let the
sea;   yet how si - lent - ly   you suf - fered,   that the
own;   from each tribe and tongue and   na - tion   you are

Refrain

land   and seas   re - joice.   You're the   au - thor of   cre -
guilt - y may   go   free.   You're the au - thor of   cre -
lead - ing sin - ners   home.

a - tion,   you're the Lord   of ev - ery - one,   and your

WORDS: Keith Getty and Stuart Townend
MUSIC: Keith Getty and Stuart Townend

ACROSS THE LANDS
87.87 D with Refrain

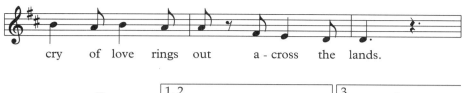

cry of love rings out a - cross the lands.

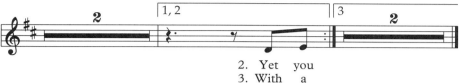

2. Yet you
3. With a

God of Great and God of Small 3033

1. God of great and God of small, God of one and
2. God of land and sky and sea, God of life and
3. God of si - lence, God of sound, God by whom the
4. God of heaven and God of earth, God of death and

God of all, God of weak and God of strong,
des - ti - ny, God of nev - er - end - ing power,
lost are found, God of day and dark - est night,
God of birth, God of now and days be - fore,

Refrain

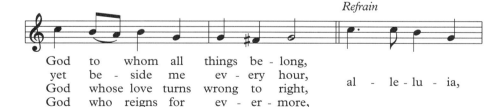

God to whom all things be - long,
yet be - side me ev - ery hour,
God whose love turns wrong to right,
God who reigns for ev - er - more,

al - le - lu - ia,

1, 2, 3   4

al - le - lu - ia, praise be to your name.

name.

WORDS: Natalie Sleeth
MUSIC: Natalie Sleeth
© 1973 Carl Fischer, Inc.

GOD OF GREAT AND SMALL
77.77 with Refrain

3034

God of Wonders

1. Lord of all creation, _ of water, earth, and _ sky,
2. Early in the morning I will celebrate the _ light,

the heavens are your tabernacle;
_ when I stumble in the darkness

glory to the Lord on _ high.
I will call your name by _ night.

Refrain

God of wonders beyond our galaxy, you are holy, holy!

The universe declares your majesty;

Last time to Coda ⊕

you are holy, holy!

1
Lord of heaven and earth, _ Lord of heaven and earth. _

2
Lord of heaven and earth. _ Hallelujah to the

WORDS: Marc Byrd and Steve Hindalong
MUSIC: Marc Byrd and Steve Hindalong

GOD OF WONDERS
Irr. with Refrain

Lord of heav-en and earth. _ Hal-le-lu - jah to the

Lord of heav-en and earth. _ Hal-le-lu - jah to the

D.S. al Coda

Lord of heav en - and earth. _ you are

CODA

Repeat as desired

Ho - ly, ho - ly!

Bless Christ through Whom All Things Are Made   3035

1., 5. Bless Christ through whom   all things are made.   Join
2. Who makes the li - on and the lamb, the
3. Who made the ore for blood-soaked nails? Who
4. Who makes the wa - ters of our birth? Who

seen and un - seen in their praise of One who both cre -
far - thest star, the small - est hand, do - min - ions, rul - ers,
made the thorns and whip-ping tails? Who made the sun that
makes the dust where we re - turn? Who makes the way for

ates, sus - tains, who goes be - fore, in jus - tice reigns.
and their powers, the stead-fast mount, the fleet - ing hours?
would not shine and made the tree on which Christ died?
us to die and rise to ev - er - last - ing life?

WORDS: Lisa Ann Moss Degrenia (Col. 1:15-18)   POXON
MUSIC: Jim Strathdee   LM
Words © 2000 Lisa Ann Moss Degrenia; music © 1998 Desert Flower Music

3036 There's No One in This World Like Jesus
(Hakuna Wakaita sa Jesu)

There's no one in this world like Je - sus, there's
Ha - ku - na wa - kai - ta sa Je - su, ha -

no one in this world like him; there's no one in this world like
ku - na wa - kai - ta sa - ye; ha - ku - na wa - kai - ta sa

Je - sus, there's no one, there's no one like him.
Je - su, ha - ku, ha - ku - chi - na.

WORDS: Traditional Shona, Zimbabwe; English trans. by Patrick Matsikenyiri and
       Daniel Charles Damon
MUSIC: Traditional Shona, Zimbabwe; arr. by Patrick Matsikenyiri

HAKUNA WAKAITA
Irr.

Trans. and arr. © 2006 Abingdon Press, admin. by The Copyright Company

3037

I Thank You, Jesus

1. I thank you, Je - sus. I thank you,
2. You've been my moth - er, you've been my

1. I thank you, Je - sus.
2. You've been my moth - er,

Je - sus. I thank you,
fa - ther, you've been my

I thank you, Je - sus. Je - sus, I thank you
you've been my fa - ther, sis - ter, my broth - er

Lord, oh, you brought me, yes, you brought me from a
too,

might - y, a might - y long way, a might - y long

WORDS: Kenneth Morris
MUSIC: Kenneth Morris, arr. by Joseph Joubert

I THANK YOU
Irr.

3038

Mighty to Save

WORDS: Ben Fielding and Reuben Morgan
MUSIC: Ben Fielding and Reuben Morgan, arr. by Jay Rouse

MIGHTY TO SAVE
Irr.

con-quered the grave.

Shine your light and let the whole world _ see we're sing-ing

for the glo - ry of the ris - en _____ King. Je - sus!

King. Sav-ior, he can move the moun-tains; my God is

might-y to save, he is might-y to save. For -

ev - er, Au-thor of sal - va - tion, he rose and

con-quered the grave, Je - sus con-quered the grave. You're my

Sav - ior. You can move the moun - tains; God, you are

might - y to save, you are might-y to save. For -

ev - er, Au-thor of sal - va - tion, you rose and

con-quered the grave; yes, you con-quered the grave. ____

You are might-y to save. __

3039   Jesus, the Saving Name

1. Je - sus, the sav - ing Name! As - cen - ded, glo - ri -
2. (E) - ter - nal Lord most high, and with the Fa - ther
3. (Sal) - va - tion's source and strength! In Je - sus' Name we
4. (Un) - wea - ried grace di - vine to take the sin - ner's
5. (So) lift on high his praise, the Sav - ior's love pro -

fied, he reigns who once for sin - ners came, and
one! His Name an - gel - ic voic - es cry, the
prove the depth and breadth and height and length of
part! May Je - sus' Name in glo - ry shine on
claim, and all the songs of all our days be

1-4

once for sin - ners died. 2. E -
ev - er - last - ing Son. 3. Sal -
God's re - deem - ing love. 4. Un -
ev - ery con - trite heart. 5. So

5

"Glo - ry to his Name!"

WORDS: Timothy Dudley-Smith
MUSIC: Jane Marshall

TWENTY
SM

You Are My All in All

3040

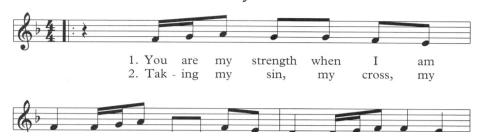

1. You are my strength when I am
2. Tak - ing my sin, my cross, my

weak. You are the treas-ure that I seek. You are my all in
shame, ris - ing a - gain I bless your name, you are my all in

all. Seek-ing you as a pre - cious
all. When I fall down you pick me

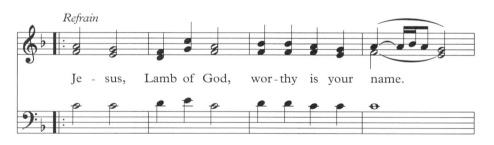

jewel, Lord, to give up I'd be a fool. You are my all in all.
up. When I am dry you fill my cup. You are my all in all.

Refrain

Je - sus, Lamb of God, wor-thy is your name.

Je - sus, Lamb of God, wor-thy is your name. name.

*Verses and refrain may be sung at the same time.

WORDS: Dennis Jernigan
MUSIC: Dennis Jernigan, arr. by William S. Moon

ALL IN ALL
885.885 with Refrain

3041

Praise Him

Refrain

1., 3. Praise him!   Praise him!   _ Praise him! _____
2. Glo - ry!   Glo - ry!   In all things give him

Praise him!   Je - sus, bless-ed Sav - ior, he's
glo - ry.

1, 2 To stanzas | *3*   *Fine*

wor - thy to be praised.   praised.

Stanza

1. From the ris - ing of the sun un - til the

WORDS: Donnie Harper
MUSIC: Donnie Harper

PRAISE HIM
Irr.

3042 Shout to the North

St. 1 - Men or All
St. 2 - Women or All
St. 3 - All

1. Men of faith, rise up and sing of the
(2. Rise up,) wo - men of the truth, stand and
(3. Rise up,) church with bro - ken wings, fill this

great and glo - rious king. You are strong when you feel
sing to bro - ken hearts who can know the heal - ing
place with songs a - gain of our God who reigns on

Third Time to Coda
(Final Refrain)

weak in your bro - ken - ness com - plete.
power of our awe - some king of love.
high. By his grace a - gain we'll fly.

Refrain
All

Shout to the north and the south, sing to the

east and the west. Je - sus is Sav - ior to all,

[1] *Repeat to Stanza 2*

Lord of heav - en and earth. 2. Rise up,

[2] *Repeat to Refrain D.S.* [3] *To Bridge* *Bridge*

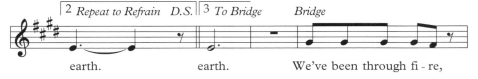

earth. earth. We've been through fi - re,

WORDS: Martin Smith
MUSIC: Martin Smith

SHOUT TO THE NORTH
Irr.

3043 You, Lord, Are Both Lamb and Shepherd

1. You, Lord, are both Lamb and Shep - herd.
2. Clothed in light up - on the moun - tain,
3. You, who walk each day be - side us,
4. Wor - thy is our earth - ly Je - sus!

You, Lord, are both prince and slave.
stripped of might up - on the cross,
sit in pow - er at God's side.
Wor - thy is our cos - mic Christ!

You, peace - mak - er and sword - bring - er
shin - ing in e - ter - nal glo - ry,
You, who preach the way that's nar - row,
Wor - thy your de - feat and vic - tory.

of the way you took and gave.
beg - gar'd by a sol - dier's toss,
have a love that reach - es wide.
Wor - thy still your peace and strife.

You, the ev - er - last - ing in -
You, the ev - er - last - ing in -
You, the ev - er - last - ing in -
You, the ev - er - last - ing in -

stant; you, whom we both scorn and crave.
stant; you, who are both gift and cost.
stant; you, who are our pil - grim guide.
stant; you, who are our death and life.

WORDS: Sylvia Dunstan
MUSIC: French Carol

PICARDY
87.87.87

Make Way

1. Make way, make way, for Christ the King in splen - dor ar - rives.
2. He comes the bro - ken hearts to heal, the pris - oners to free.

Fling wide the gates and wel - come him in - to your lives.
The deaf shall hear, the lame shall dance, the blind shall see.

Refrain

Part 1

Make way, make way for the

Part 2

Make way, make way

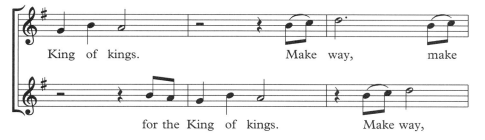

King of kings. Make way, make

for the King of kings. Make way,

way and let his king - dom in.

make way and let his king - dom in.

WORDS: Graham Kendrick
MUSIC: Graham Kendrick

MAKE WAY
86.84 with Refrain

3045

Down by the Jordan

1. Down by the Jor - dan, a proph - et named John was bap -
2. There by the riv - er, the crowd came with great ex - pec -
3. Je - sus, you went to be bap - tized a - long with the
4. Here in the Church, we are bap - tized and filled with God's

tiz - ing, preach - ing a mes - sage the
ta - tion: "Are you God's Cho - sen One,
oth - ers, tak - ing your place a - mong
Spir - it. Freed and for - giv - en we're

peo - ple found bold and sur - pris - ing.
sent here to res - cue our na - tion?"
sin - ners, God's lost sons and daugh - ters.
wel - comed with joy! Can you hear it?

"God will for - give! Show that you'll change how you
"No!" John re - plied. "He who is might - ier than
Then with great love, God's Spir - it came as a
This is God's sign! This is how God says, "You're

WORDS: Carolyn Winfrey Gillette
MUSIC: *Erneuerten Gesangbuch*, 1665; harm. by William Sterndale Bennett

LOBE DEN HERREN
14 14.478

Come, O Redeemer, Come 3046

live! Sure - ly God's new day is ris - ing!"
I judg - es and of - fers sal - va - tion."
dove! Your work be - gan in those wa - ters.
mine!" Let's take the good news and share it!

1. Fa - ther, en-throned on high, ho ly, - ho ly;
2. Lord, save us from the dark of our striv - ing,
3. Look now up - on our need, Lord, be with us.

|1|

an - cient e - ter - nal Light, hear our prayer. _____
faith - less and trou-bled hearts, weighed
Heal us and make us free from our

|2, 3| *Refrain*

down. _____ Come, O Re-deem-er, come, grant us
sin. _____

Last time to Coda ⊕   *D.S. al Coda*

mer-cy. Come, O Re-deem-er, come, grant us peace. ___

⊕ CODA

grant us peace. _____

WORDS: Fernando Ortega
MUSIC: Fernando Ortega
© 1996 IzzySolSongs, admin. by Metro One

ORTEGA
64.63 with Refrain

3047 God Almighty, We Are Waiting

1. God Almighty, we are waiting
2. God Incarnate, we are waiting
3. God the Spirit, we are waiting

1. for a Savior to appear.
2. for the feast day of your birth.
3. for your presence here and now.

1. Meet us in our desert journey;
2. Looking back and looking forward
3. Humbled by our sinful weakness,

1. give a sign that you are near:
2. to the Christ's return to earth.
3. at your mercy we will bow.

WORDS: Ann Bell Worley
MUSIC: Rowland Prichard; harm. from *The English Hymnal*, 1906
Words © 2005 Hope Publishing Company

HYFRYDOL
87.87 D

burn - ing bush - es, part - ed wa - ters,
Help us to pro - claim the gos - pel,
Search our hearts and make us read - y,

food a plen - ty in the wild.
'til the world is rec - on - ciled.
speak in lan - guage strong and mild,

As we look for signs and won - ders,
Let us set your ho - ly ta - ble
help each one of us, your peo - ple,

help us see you in a child.
for each wo - man, man, and child.
to re - ceive you like a child.

3048 View the Present through the Promise

1. View the pres-ent through the prom-ise, Christ will come a - gain.
2. Probe the pres-ent with the prom-ise, Christ will come a - gain.
3. Match the pres-ent to the prom-ise, Christ will come a - gain.

Trust de-spite the deep-ening dark-ness, Christ will come a - gain.
Let your dai - ly ac - tions wit - ness, Christ will come a - gain.
Make this hope your guid - ing prem-ise, Christ will come a - gain.

Lift the world a - bove its griev-ing through your watch-ing and be-liev-ing
Let your lov-ing and your giv - ing and your jus - tice and for-giv-ing
Pat-tern all your cal - cu - lat-ing and the world you are cre - a - ting

in the hope past hope's con-ceiv-ing: Christ will come a - gain.
be a sign to all the liv-ing: Christ will come a - gain.
to the ad - vent you are wait-ing: Christ will come a - gain.

WORDS: Thomas H. Troeger   AR HYD Y NOS (alt.)
MUSIC: Traditional Welsh melody; harm. by Luther Orlando Emerson   85.85.888.5

Wait for the Lord

Wait for the Lord, whose day is near.

Wait for the Lord: keep watch, take heart!

WORDS: Jacques Berthier (Ps. 27:14)
MUSIC: Jacques Berthier

WAIT FOR THE LORD
44.44

Until Jesus Comes

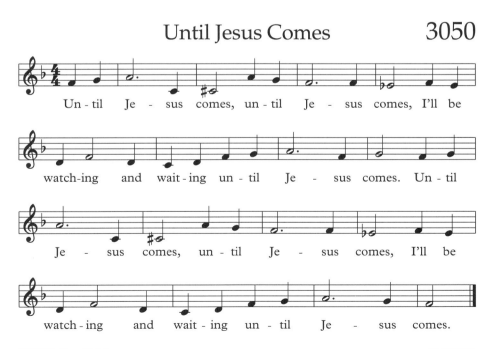

Un - til Je - sus comes, un - til Je - sus comes, I'll be

watch-ing and wait-ing un - til Je - sus comes. Un - til

Je - sus comes, un - til Je - sus comes, I'll be

watch-ing and wait-ing un - til Je - sus comes.

WORDS: Dean McIntyre
MUSIC: Dean McIntyre

PAROUSIA
55.75 D

3051

A Star Shone Bright

1. A star shone bright a-cross the plain and calmed the
2. O Son of God, In-car-nate Word, O Wis-dom's
3. From Beth-le-hem come to our day; re-veal to
4. O star shine forth once more this night and flood our

earth so Love could reign. 'Twas in a child that hope was
Light, whom an-gels heard, come forth a-gain, our hearts con-
us your ho-ly way. Be born a-gain, E-ter-nal
streets with heaven-ly Light till ev-ery heart in Christ shall

born, a dream ful-filled! O hap-py morn!
sole. O heal our hurts and make us whole.
Fire. O Spir-it come, our souls in-spire.
see the glo-ry of e-ter-ni-ty!

WORDS: F. Richard Garland
MUSIC: English folk melody; harm. by Dean McIntyre

O WALY WALY
LM

God Rest You Merry, Gentlemen 3052

1. God rest you mer - ry, gen - tle-men, let noth-ing you dis - may,
2. In Beth - le - hem in Ju - dah this bless-ed babe was born,
3. From God our heaven-ly Fa - ther a bless-ed an - gel came,
4. The shep-herds at those tid - ings re - joic-ed much in mind,
5. Now to the Lord sing prais - es, all you with - in this place,

for Je - sus Christ our Sav - ior was born up - on this day,
and laid with - in a man - ger up - on this bless - ed morn:
and un - to cer - tain shep - herds brought tid - ings of the same,
and left their flocks a - feed - ing in tem-pest, storm, and wind,
and with true love and broth-er-hood each oth - er now em - brace;

to save us all from Sa - tan's power when we were gone a - stray.
for which his moth-er Ma - ry did noth-ing take in scorn.
how that in Beth-le - hem was born the Son of God by name.
and went to Beth-le - hem straight-way, the bless-ed babe to find.
this ho - ly tide of Christ - mas all oth - ers doth de - face.

Refrain

O tid - ings of com - fort and joy, com-fort and

joy; O tid - ings of com - fort and joy.

WORDS: Traditional English carol, 18th cent.
MUSIC: Traditional English melody

GOD REST YOU MERRY
Irr. with Refrain

3053   Bethlehem

Refrain

Beth - le - hem, _ Beth - le - hem, _ cit - y where _

_ the King was born. _ Beth - le - hem, _ Beth - le - hem, _

Fine

_ Ma - ry had - a Je - sus on Christ - mas morn. _

Leader   *All*

1. Ma - ry, Ma - ry, meek and mild; ____ Ma - ry had - a
2. Jo - seph took Ma - ry by the hand, ____ Ma - ry had - a
3. Ma - ry put Je - sus in the hay. ____ Ma - ry had - a

Leader

Je - sus on Christ - mas morn. _ Moth - er of ____ the
Je - sus on Christ - mas morn. _ Trav - el - ing ____ through -
Je - sus on Christ - mas morn. _ That was his bed ____ on

All   *D.C. al Fine*

Ho - ly Child. ___ Ma - ry had - a Je - sus on Christ - mas morn. _
out the land. ___ Ma - ry had - a Je - sus on Christ - mas morn. _
Christ - mas Day. ___ Ma - ry had - a Je - sus on Christ - mas morn. _

WORDS: Marilyn E. Thornton   BETHLEHEM
MUSIC: Marilyn E. Thornton   Irr. with Refrain

© 1985 Marilyn E. Thornton

3054   Chinese Lantern Carol

1. Ti - ny hand strike ti - ny chime! Chil - dren all in a row
2. Bow to gen - tle Ma - ry mild, bow to Jo - seph, so,
3. All your wor - ry, hun - ger, and pain be for - got - ten to - night;

WORDS: Jacqueline Hanna McNair   LANTERN STAR
MUSIC: Chinese folk melody   Irr.

Words © 1989 Kirkland House Music

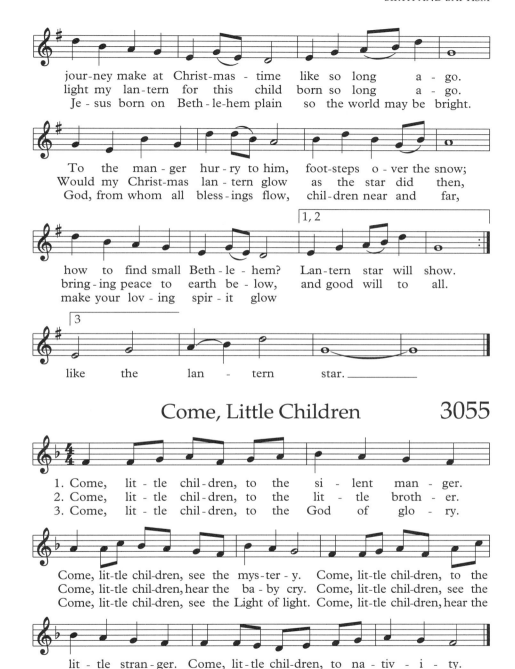

jour-ney make at Christ-mas - time   like so long   a - go.
light my lan-tern for this   child   born so long   a - go.
Je - sus born on Beth - le-hem plain   so the world may be bright.

To   the   man - ger   hur - ry to him,   foot-steps   o - ver the snow;
Would my Christ-mas   lan - tern glow   as   the star did   then,
God, from whom all   bless - ings flow,   chil-dren near and   far,

[1, 2]

how   to   find small   Beth - le - hem?   Lan-tern star will   show.
bring - ing peace to   earth be - low,   and good will   to   all.
make your lov - ing   spir - it   glow

[3]

like   the   lan - tern   star.

Come, Little Children   3055

1. Come,   lit - tle   chil - dren, to   the   si - lent   man - ger.
2. Come,   lit - tle   chil - dren, to   the   lit - tle   broth - er.
3. Come,   lit - tle   chil - dren, to   the   God   of   glo - ry.

Come, lit-tle chil-dren, see the mys-ter - y.   Come, lit-tle chil-dren, to the
Come, lit-tle chil-dren, hear the ba - by cry.   Come, lit-tle chil-dren, see the
Come, lit-tle chil-dren, see the Light of light.   Come, lit-tle chil-dren, hear the

lit - tle stran - ger.   Come, lit - tle chil-dren, to na - tiv - i - ty.
Ma - ry moth - er.   Come, lit - tle chil-dren, see the star   on high.
gos - pel sto - ry.   Come, lit - tle chil-dren, it is Christ-mas night.

WORDS: Herbert Brokering, Robert Sterling, and Rusty Edwards
MUSIC: Herbert Brokering, Robert Sterling, and Rusty Edwards

HOWARD
11 10.11 10

3056 Jesus, the Light of the World

1. See the bright and Morn-ing Star, Je-sus, the Light of the
2. He's the lamp that lights our way, Je-sus, the Light of the
3. No more dark - ness, no more night — Je-sus, the Light of the

World! He has ris - en in our hearts, Je-sus, the Light of the
World! Step by step and day by day — Je-sus, the Light of the
World! He will shine for - ev - er bright, Je-sus, the Light of the

Refrain

World!
World! Walk in the light, beau - ti - ful light;
World!

come where his love and his mer-cy are bright. Shine all a-round us by

WORDS: Ken Bible and George D. Elderkin
MUSIC: Ken Bible and George D. Elderkin

ELDERKIN
77.77 with Refrain

day and by night, Je - sus, the Light of the World.

Glory in the Highest   3057
(*Gloria en las alturas*)

1. Glo - ry   in   the   high - est   and peace   on   the   earth!
2. Je - sus seeks no   lodg - ing   that   sets   him   a - part;
1. *Glo-ria en las   al - tu - ras   y en   la   tie - rra paz!*
2. *Je - sús   ya   no   quie - re   po - sa - da en   me - són;*

Glo - ry   in   the   high - est   and peace   on   the   earth!   Sing
Je - sus seeks no   lodg - ing   that   sets   him   a - part;   He
Glo-ria en las   al - tu - ras   y en   la   tie - rra paz!   *Di -*
Je - sús   ya   no   quie - re   po - sa - da en   me - són.   *El*

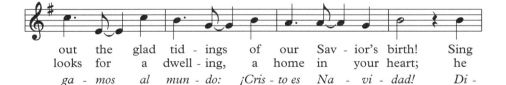

out   the   glad   tid - ings   of   our   Sav - ior's birth!   Sing
looks   for   a   dwell - ing,   a   home   in   your heart;   he
ga - mos   al   mun - do: ¡Cris - to es   Na - vi - dad!   *Di -*
bus - ca   mo - ra - da   en   tu   co - ra - zón.   *El*

out   the   glad   tid - ings   of   our   Sav - ior's birth!
looks   for   a   dwell - ing,   a   home   in   your heart.
ga - mos   al   mun - do: ¡Cris - to es   Na - vi - dad!
bus - ca   mo - ra - da   en   tu   co - ra - zón.

WORDS: Traditional Puerto Rican; English trans. by Gerhard Cartford
MUSIC: Traditional Puerto Rican; arr. by Raquel Mora Martínez

GLORIA
65.65 D

Trans. © 1998 Augsburg Fortress; arr. © 2004 Raquel Mora Martínez

3058

Mary Had a Baby

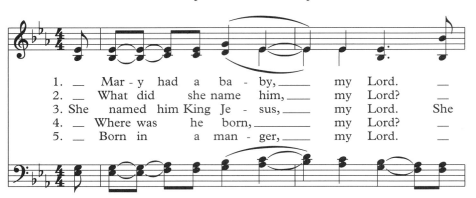

1. __ Mar - y had a ba - by, ____ my Lord. __
2. __ What did she name him, ____ my Lord? __
3. She named him King Je - sus, ____ my Lord. She
4. __ Where was he born, ____ my Lord? __
5. __ Born in a man - ger, ____ my Lord. __

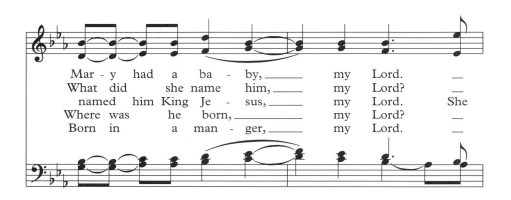

Mar - y had a ba - by, ____ my Lord. __
What did she name him, ____ my Lord? __
named him King Je - sus, ____ my Lord. She
Where was he born, ____ my Lord? __
Born in a man - ger, ____ my Lord. __

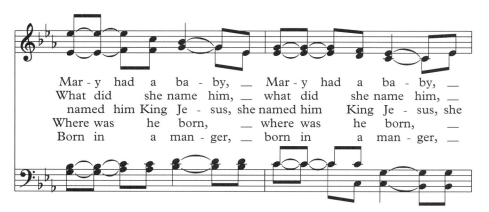

Mar - y had a ba - by, __ Mar - y had a ba - by, __
What did she name him, __ what did she name him, __
named him King Je - sus, she named him King Je - sus, she
Where was he born, __ where was he born, __
Born in a man - ger, __ born in a man - ger, __

WORDS: African American spiritual
MUSIC: African American spiritual; arr. by Kenneth L. Fenton

MARY HAD A BABY
Irr.

Arr. © 1996 Kenneth Fenton

Mar - y had a ba - by, ____ my Lord.
what did she name him, ____ my Lord?
named him King Je - sus, ____ my Lord.
where was he born, ____ my Lord?
born in a man - ger, ____ my Lord.

Love Has Come 3059

1. Love has come — a light in the dark - ness! Love shines
2. Love is born! Come, share in the won - der. Love is
3. Love has come and nev - er will leave us! Love is

forth in the Beth - le - hem skies. See, all heav - en has
God now a - sleep in the hay. See the glow in the
life ev - er - last - ing and free. Love is Je - sus with -

come to pro - claim it; hear how their song of joy a -
eyes of his moth - er; what is the name her heart is
in and a - mong us. Love is the peace our hearts are

ris - es: Love! Love! Born un - to you, a Sav - ior!
say - ing? Love! Love! Love is the name she whis - pers.
seek - ing. Love! Love! Love is the gift of Christ - mas.

Love! Love! Glo - ry to God on high. ____
Love! Love! Je - sus, Im - man - u - el. ____
Love! Love! Praise to you, God on high! ____

WORDS: Ken Bible
MUSIC: Traditional French
Words © 1996 LNWhymns.com, admin. by Music Services

BRING A TORCH
9 9.10 9.9 8

3060 Jesus, Jesus, Oh, What a Wonderful Child

Je-sus, Je-sus, oh, what a won-der-ful child. Je-sus, Je-sus, so ho-ly, meek and mild; new life, new hope the child will bring. Lis-ten to the an-gel sing, "Glo-ry, glo-ry, glo-ry," let the heav-ens ring.

WORDS: Traditional African American
MUSIC: Traditional African American; arr. by Jeffrey Radford

WONDERFUL CHILD
Irr.

Arr. © 1992 The Pilgrim Press

See Him Lying on a Bed of Straw   3061

1. See him ly - ing on a bed of straw: a
2. Star of sil - ver, sweep a - cross the skies, —
3. An - gels, sing a - gain the song you sang, —
4. Mine are rich - es, from your pov - er - ty, —

draft - y sta - ble with an o - pen door;
show where Je - sus in the man - ger lies;
sing the glo - ry of God's gra - cious plan;
from your in - no - cence, e - ter - ni - ty;

Ma - ry cra - dl - ing the babe she bore — the
shep - herds, swift - ly from your stu - por rise to
sing that Beth - lehem's lit - tle ba - by can —
mine, for - give - ness by your death for me, —

Refrain

Prince of glo - ry is his name.
see the Sav - ior of the world!
be the Sav - ior of us all.   Oh, now car - ry me to
Child of sor - row for my joy.

Beth - le - hem   to   see the Lord   of love a - gain:

|1-3
just as poor as was the sta - ble then, the Prince of glo - ry when he

|4
came. —   sta - ble then, the Prince of glo - ry when he came. —

WORDS: Michael Perry
MUSIC: Michael Perry; arr. by Stephen Coates

CALYPSO CAROL
Irr.

3062 Spirit-Child Jesus

1. Spir-it-child Je-sus, in joy-ful re-frain, ech-o-ing
2. Spir-it-child Je-sus, in an-i-mal shed, smil-ing at
3. Spir-it-child Je-sus, in star-ry white light, twin-kling on
4. Spir-it-child Je-sus, in vig-i-lant eyes, wait-ing the
5. Spir-it-child Je-sus, in hot tongues of flame, melt-ing the

songs o-ver Beth-le-hem's plain, what will we do when the
shep-herds from strange bor-rowed bed, what will we do when the
ev-er-greens, shin-y and bright, what will we do when the
gift bear-ing Love's great sur-prise, what will we do when the
can-dle a-light in your name, what will we do when the

car-ols all fade? "Take up my song: Glo-ry! Be not a-fraid!"
man-ger's a-way? "Take up my sto-ry, and live it each day!"
branch-es are shorn? "Take up my cross that for you I have borne!"
pres-ents are done? "Take up my pres-ence, for I am God's Son!"
can-dle is gone? "Take up my light! Pass it on, pass it on!"

WORDS: Mary Nelson Keithahn
MUSIC: John D. Horman

SPIRIT-CHILD
10 10.10 10

© 1997 Abingdon Press, admin. by The Copyright Company

3063 If I Could Visit Bethlehem

1. If I could vis-it Beth-le-hem what pres-ents would I bring? If
2. I'd learn some sim-ple words to speak in Ar-a-ma-ic tongues. I'd
3. I'd say, "He'll nev-er hurt or kill, and joy will fol-low tears. We'll

I could see what hap-pened then, what would I say or sing? I
cra-dle him, and kiss his cheek, and say, "I'm glad you've come." If
know his name and love him still in twen-ty hun-dred years." I

WORDS: Brian Wren
MUSIC: Hal H. Hopson

CAROL STREAM
CMD

Words © 1990, music © 1996 Hope Publishing Company

would-n't take a   mod-ern toy but gold to pay   for bread, some
Ma - ry asked me   who I was and what her child would do,   I
can - not vis - it   Beth-le-hem but what I can, I'll do: I'll

wine to give his   par-ents joy   and wool to warm his   bed. ____
would-n't talk a - bout the cross   or   tell her all   I   knew. ____
love you, Je - sus, as my friend, and give my life to   you. ____

On Christmas Night 3064

1. On Christ-mas night all   Chris-tians sing, to   hear the news   the
2. Then why should we   on   earth be sad, since our Re-deem - er
3. When sin   de-parts be - fore   his grace, then life and health come
4. All out   of dark-ness we   have light, which made the an - gels

an - gels bring. On Christ-mas night all   Chris-tians sing,   to
made us glad. Then why should we   on   earth be sad, since
in   its place. When sin   de-parts be - fore   his grace, then
sing this night. All   out   of dark-ness we   have light, which

hear the news   the an-gels bring: news of great joy, news of great
our Re-deem - er made us glad; when from our sin   he set us
life and health come in its place; heav - en and   earth with joy may
made the an - gels sing this night: "Glo - ry to   God, on earth be

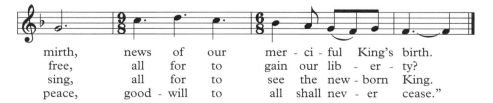

mirth,   news   of   our   mer - ci - ful King's birth.
free,   all   for   to   gain our lib - er - ty?
sing,   all   for   to   see   the new - born King.
peace,   good - will   to   all   shall nev - er cease."

WORDS: Traditional English
MUSIC: Traditional English melody

SUSSEX CAROL
LM

3065 Some Children See Him

1. Some chil - dren see him lil - y white, the
2. Some chil - dren see him al - mond - eyed, this
3. The chil - dren in each dif - ferent place will

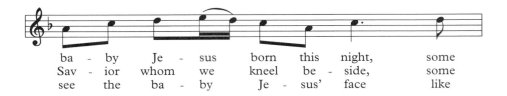

ba - by Je - sus born this night, some
Sav - ior whom we kneel be - side, some
see the ba - by Je - sus' face like

chil - dren see him lil - y white, with tress - es soft and fair.
chil - dren see him al - mond-eyed, with skin of yel - low hue.
theirs, but bright with heaven-ly grace, and filled with ho - ly light.

Some chil - dren see him bronzed and brown, the
Some chil - dren see him dark as they, sweet
O lay a - side each earth - ly thing, and

Lord of heaven to earth come down; some
Ma - ry's Son to whom we pray; some
with thy heart as of - fer - ing, come

chil-dren see him bronzed and brown, with dark and heav-y hair.
chil-dren see him dark as they, and ah! they love him, too!
wor-ship now the in - fant King. 'Tis love that's born to - night!

WORDS: Wihla Hutson
MUSIC: Alfred Burt

SOME CHILDREN
86.86 D

Still, Still, Still

1. Still, still, still, the night is cold and chill. The vir-gin's ten-der arms en-fold-ing, warm and safe the Christ child hold-ing. Still, still, still, the night is cold and chill.

2. Dream, dream, dream, he sleeps, the Sav-ior king. While guard-ian an-gels watch be-side him Ma-ry ten-der-ly will guide him. Dream, dream, dream, he sleeps, the Sav-ior king.

3. *Schlaf, schlaf, schlaf, mein lie-bes Kind-lein, schlaf. Die Eng-el tun schön mu-si-zier-en, bei dem Kind-lein ju-bi-lier-en. Schlaf, schlaf, schlaf, mein lie-bes Kind-lein, schlaf.*

WORDS: Traditional Austrian carol
MUSIC: Melody from *Salzburger Volkslieder*; arr. by Dean McIntyre

STILL, STILL, STILL
99.89

BIRTH AND BAPTISM

3067 Welcome to Our World

1. __ Tears are fall - ing, hearts are break - ing;
2. __ Hope that you don't mind our man - ger,
3. __ Bring your peace in - to our vi - o-lence,
4. __ Frag - ile fin - ger sent to heal us,
(5. So) wrap our in - jured flesh a - round you,

how we need to hear from God. __ You've been prom - ised,
how I wish we would have known. but long a - wait - ed
bid our hun-gry souls be filled. __ Word now break - ing
ten - der brow pre-pared for thorn, __ ti - ny heart whose
breathe our air and walk our sod. __ Rob our sin and

we've been wait - ing, wel-come ho - ly Child, __ __
ho - ly stran-ger, make your-self at home, __ please
heav - en's si - lence, wel-come to our world, __ __
blood will save us, un - to us is born, __ __
make us ho - ly, per - fect Son of God, __ __

1-4

wel-come ho - ly Child. ____ 2. __
make your-self at home. ____ 3. __
wel-come to our world. ____ 4. __
un - to us is born. ____ 5. So

5 _____ rit.

per - fect Son of God. _____ Wel-come to our

a tempo

world. _____

WORDS: Chris Rice
MUSIC: Chris Rice

WELCOME TO OUR WORLD
Irr.

The Lord's Prayer

WORDS: Based on Matt. 6:9-13
MUSIC: Albert Malotte

MALOTTE
Irr.

Music © 1935 (renewed) G. Schirmer, Inc. (BMI)

3069

The Lord's Prayer
(Padre nuestro)

Our Fa - ther,____ Fa - ther in heav - en,_____
Pa-dre nues - tro_____ que es-tás en el cie - lo,_____

hal - low-ed be, hal - low-ed be, thy name.
san - ti - fi - ca-do, san - ti - fi - ca-do, se - a tu nom-bre.

Fine

2

1. Your king - dom come, _____
2. Give us to - day our dai - ly
3. __ Save us from the time of
1. __ *Vén - ga nos tu rei - no, Se -*
2. __ *Da - nos hoy, dá - nos - lo, Se -*
3. __ *No nos de - jes ca - er en ten - ta -*

__ your will be done_____
bread. For - give us our sins____
trial and de - liv - er us from e -
ñor; _____ há - ga - se tu san - ta vo - lun -
ñor, _____ nues - tro pan, el pan de ca - da
ción; _____ an - tes bien, lí - bra - nos del

____ on earth_____ as it
____ as we for - give those who
vil. For the king-dom, power, and glo - ry are yours
tad en el cie - lo y en la tie - rra. Ha - re - mos tu
dí - a y per - do - na nues - tras deu - das a - sí co - mo no -
mal. Por-que tu - yo es el rei - no, tu - yo el po -

WORDS: Based on Matt. 6:9-13; Spanish trans. by Carlos Rosas;
English adapt. by Dean McIntyre
MUSIC: Carlos Rosas

PADRE NUESTRO
Irr. with Refrain

Spanish trans. and music © 1976 Carlos Rosas, admin. by OCP; English adaptation © 2001 The General Board of Discipleship of The United Methodist Church.

D.S.

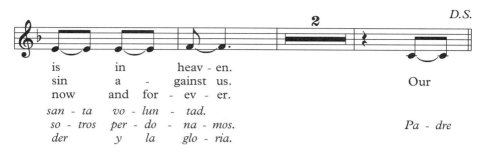

is   in   heav - en.
sin   a - gainst us.
now   and for - ev - er.
san - ta   vo - lun - tad.
so - tros per - do - na - mos.
der   y   la   glo - ria.

Our

Pa - dre

The Lord's Prayer

3070

Our Fa - ther in heav - en, hal-low-ed be your name. Your king-dom come, your will be done on earth as in heav - en. Give us to - day our dai - ly bread. For-give us our sins as we for - give those who sin a - gainst us. ____ Save us from the time of trial and de-liv-er us from e - vil, for the king - dom, the power, and the glo - ry are yours, now and for - ev - er. ____

WORDS: Based on Matt. 6:9-13
MUSIC: David Haas

LORD'S PRAYER (HAAS)
Irr.

Music © 1986 GIA Publications

3071 The Lord's Prayer

Our God in heav-en, ho-ly is your

name, your reign come, your will done, on earth as in

heav-en. Give us to-day our dai - ly bread, and

molto rit.

help us for - give, as we have been for - giv - en.

a tempo

In the time of tri - al lead us in - to light, for

yours is the king-dom, and the pow-er, and the glo-ry, for -

WORDS: Matt. 6:9-13; adapt. by Mark A. Miller and Laurie Zelman
MUSIC: Mark A. Miller

LORD'S PRAYER (MILLER)
Irr.

Cast Out, O Christ 3072

1. Cast out, O Christ, cast far a - way the
2. Our rag - ing griefs, our jeal - ous fears are
3. Once long a - go, from Gal - i - lee, you
4. Your Word breathes life and health and hope that
5. So come, O Christ and cast a - way the

de - mons that de - stroy: the haunt - ing dreads that
Le - gion in their name. Our shack - led hearts im -
sailed to storm - tossed shores. And still, in power, you
break through e - vil's thrall. You send us, strength-ened,
de - mons that de - stroy. Trans-form our lives to

choke our souls, the hates that sti - fle joy.
plore your grace to loose our bind - ing shame.
brave new paths to breach our bolt - ed doors.
home in peace to live your gos - pel call.
sense your love and spread a - broad your joy.

WORDS: Mary Louise Bringle
MUSIC: American folk melody
Words © 2006 GIA Publications, Inc.

HOUSE OF THE RISING SUN
CM

3073

We Walk His Way

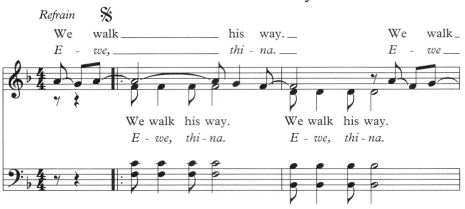

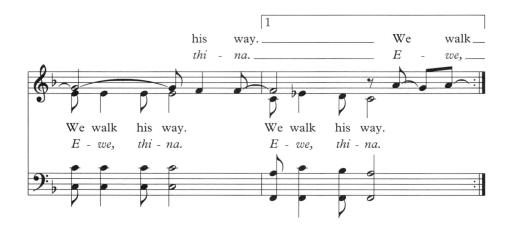

WORDS: South African; trans. by Anders Nyberg and Sven-Bernhard Fast
MUSIC: South African; arr. by Anders Nyberg

EWE THINA
Irr. with Refrain

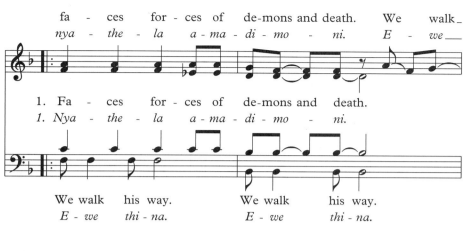

fa - ces for - ces of de-mons and death. We walk
nya - the - la a - ma - di - mo - ni. E - we

1. Fa - ces for - ces of de-mons and death.
1. Nya - the - la a - ma - di - mo - ni.

We walk his way. We walk his way.
E - we thi - na. E - we thi - na.

1

_____ his way. ___ 1. Un-armed, he
thi - na. ___ 1. Si - zo - wa

We walk his way. We walk his way.
E - we, thi - na. E - we, thi - na.

D.S. al Fine

2

_____ his way. ___ We walk
thi - na. ___ E - we

We walk his way. We walk his way.
E - we, thi - na. E - we, thi - na.

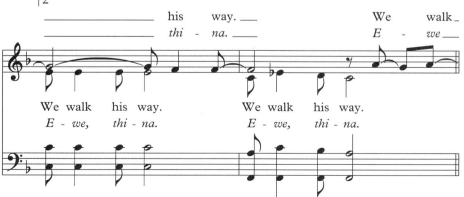

2. He breaks the bonds of hell dying on the cross,…

3. The tree of freedom blooms by his empty grave,…

3074   Jesus Is a Rock in a Weary Land

Refrain
All

Je-sus is a rock in a wea-ry land, a wea-ry land, a

wea - ry land; my Je - sus is a rock in a

Fine

wea - ry land, a shel-ter in the time of storm. _

Leader or All

1. No one can do like Je - sus, not a
2. When Je - sus was on earth_____ the
3. ___ Yon - der comes my Sav - ior, him

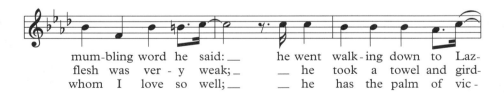

mum-bling word he said: ___ he went walk-ing down to Laz-
flesh was ver - y weak; ___ ___ he took a towel and gird-
whom I love so well; ___ ___ he has the palm of vic-

D.C.

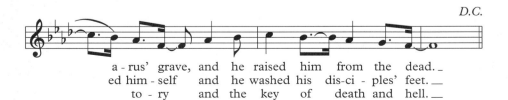

a - rus' grave, and he raised him from the dead. _
ed him - self and he washed his dis-ci - ples' feet. _
to - ry and the key of death and hell. _

WORDS: African American spiritual
MUSIC: African American spiritual

WEARY LAND
Irr. with Refrain

Glory in the Cross

1. Let us ev - er glo - ry in the cross of Christ who re -
(2. Let us) bring our bur-dens to the cross of Christ who has
(3. Let us) kneel in hom-age at the cross of Christ where we

deems us with his blood. Let us tell the sto - ry of the
known our sor-row and tears. In the great com-pas-sion of the
see God's hu - man face. We be-hold the Mak-er of the

cross of Christ and the power of his sav - ing love. Like a
heart of Christ, God has walked in our hopes and fears. He was
sun and stars as he hangs on the throne of grace. As we

lamb he was slain; he car - ried our shame, to
mocked and be-trayed, de - sert - ed by friends, and
share in his pain, his sor - row and shame, our

show us the mer-cy of God.
ban-ished to die a-mong thieves. Let us ev - er glo-ry in the
hearts will be test-ed in fire.

cross of Christ and the tri-umph of God's great love.

2. Let us   3. Let us

WORDS: Dan Schutte
MUSIC: Dan Schutte
© 2000 Daniel L. Schutte, admin. by OCP

TRIDUUM
11 8.11 8 D

3076

Ivory Palaces

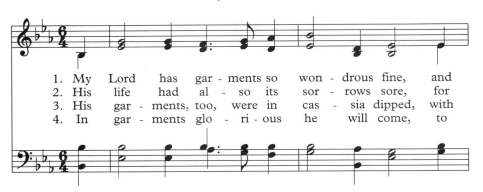

1. My Lord has gar - ments so won - drous fine, and
2. His life had al - so its sor - rows sore, for
3. His gar - ments, too, were in cas - sia dipped, with
4. In gar - ments glo - ri - ous he will come, to

myrrh their tex - ture fills; its fra - grance reached to this
al - oes had a part; and when I think of the
heal - ing in a touch; each time my feet in some
o - pen wide the door; and I shall en - ter my

heart of mine, with joy my be - ing thrills.
cross he bore, my eyes with tear - drops start.
sin have slipped, he took me from its clutch.
heaven - ly home, to dwell for - ev - er - more.

WORDS: Henry Barraclough
MUSIC: Henry Barraclough

IVORY PALACES
96.96 with Refrain

Refrain

(mel.) Out of the i - vo-ry pal - a - ces in - to a world of woe,

on - ly his great e - ter -nal love made my Sav-ior go.

Blessed Is He Who Comes in God's Name 3077

1. "Bless - ed is he who comes in God's name!"
2. As the great cit - y came in - to view
3. They did not hear him; nei - ther do we.
4. Peace is not gained through pos - ture and threat.

cried the ex - cit - ed crowd. Spread - ing their cloaks, they
Je - sus be - gan to cry. "Would that you knew the
Might is our gold - en calf. We would see Christ e -
Jus - tice is not a game. Come, Chris-tians, turn; sur -

wel - comed a King; "Peace," they said, "here and now!"
mak - ings of peace!" he ut - tered with a sigh.
quipped with a sword, not with a shep - herd's staff.
ren - der the pride; re - pent in Je - sus' name.

WORDS: John Thornburg (Luke 19:28-47)
MUSIC: Jane Marshall
© 2003 Abingdon Press, admin. by The Copyright Company

LAMENT
96.96

3078

Hosanna

Ho - san-na! Ho - san-na!

Bless-ed is he who comes in the name of the Lord. _____

Ho - san-na! Ho - san - na!

Bless - ed is he who comes in the name of the Lord. _

WORDS: Mark 11:9
MUSIC: Patrick Roaché; arr. by Evelyn Simpson-Currenton
Music © 2000 Patrick Roaché, admin. by GIA Publications, Inc.

ROACHÉ
Irr.

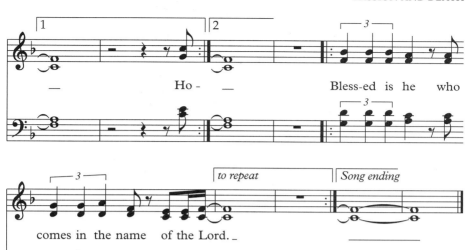

Ho - Bless-ed is he who comes in the name of the Lord.

Hosanna

3079

Leader — All — Leader

1. Ho - san - na, ho - san - na, ho - san -
2. We wel - come him, we wel - come him, we wel - come
3. We'll fol - low him, we'll fol - low him, we'll fol - low
4. We'll walk with him, we'll walk with him to Cal - va -
5. On Eas - ter morn, on Eas - ter morn we'll share the

All — Leader — All

na, ho - san - na.
him, we wel - come him.
him, we'll fol - low him. Ho - san - na, ho -
ry, to Cal - va - ry.
news, we'll share the news.

Leader and All

san - na. Ho - san - na to the King.

WORDS: Jim Strathdee
MUSIC: Jim Strathdee
© 1993 Desert Flower Music

STRATHDEE HOSANNA
Irr.

3080

Lord, Is It I?

1. Who was it who for pro - fit's gain be -
2. Who made the crown of vine and thorn? Who
3. Who fled that day so fear - ful - ly, and
4. Have I be - trayed him, mocked, or fled? Have

trayed with fond em - brace the Lamb of God to
placed it on his brow? Whose an - gry words of
who de - nied their Lord? Who chose Ba - rab - bas
I my Lord de - nied? The cross is raised, but

suf - fer pain, en - dur - ing my dis - grace? Lord,
mock and scorn are shout - ed e - ven now? Lord,
to go free? Who scourged Christ with the sword? Lord,
in my stead, is Je - sus cru - ci - fied? Lord,

WORDS: Dean McIntyre
MUSIC: Hans L. Hassler; harm. J. S. Bach
Words © 1999 Dean McIntyre

PASSION CHORALE
CMD

is it   I?   Lord,   is it   I? Am   I   the one   to   blame?   Is
is it   I?   Lord,   is it   I? Am   I   the one   to   blame?   Is
is it   I?   Lord,   is it   I? Am   I   the one   to   blame?   Is
it is   I!   Lord,   it is   I! I   am   the one   to   blame.   It

it for me   that   you must die? Is   it   for me you came?
it for me   that   you must die? Is   it   for me you came?
it for me   that   you must die? Is   it   for me you came?
is for me   you   chose to die. It   is   for me you came.

Now Behold the Lamb
3081

1. Now   be-hold   the Lamb, _   the   pre-cious Lamb   of God, _
2. Ho - ly is   the Lamb, _   the   pre-cious Lamb   of God. _
3. Thank you for the Lamb, _   the   pre-cious Lamb   of God. _

— who   bore all   my   sin   that   I   may _
— Why   you   love me   so,   Lord, I   shall _
— Be - cause of   your grace I   can   fin -

_ live a - gain: the pre-cious Lamb   of God. _
_ nev-er know;   the pre-cious Lamb   of God. _
ish the race;   the pre-cious Lamb   of God. _

WORDS: Kirk Franklin
MUSIC: Kirk Franklin

NOW BEHOLD THE LAMB
56.56.6

3082

Who Is He

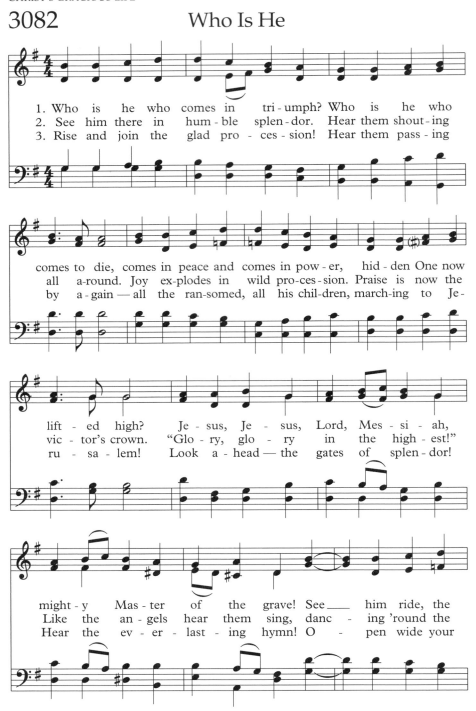

1. Who is he who comes in tri - umph? Who is he who comes to die, comes in peace and comes in pow - er, hid - den One now lift - ed high? Je - sus, Je - sus, Lord, Mes - si - ah, might - y Mas - ter of the grave! See___ him ride, the

2. See him there in hum - ble splen - dor. Hear them shout - ing all a - round. Joy ex - plodes in wild pro - ces - sion. Praise is now the vic - tor's crown. "Glo - ry, glo - ry in the high - est!" Like the an - gels hear them sing, danc - ing 'round the

3. Rise and join the glad pro - ces - sion! Hear them pass - ing by a - gain — all the ran - somed, all his chil - dren, march - ing to Je - ru - sa - lem! Look a - head — the gates of splen - dor! Hear the ev - er - last - ing hymn! O - pen wide your

WORDS: Ken Bible
MUSIC: Ludwig van Beethoven; arr. by Edward Hodges

HYMN TO JOY
87.87 D

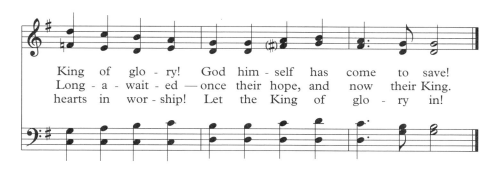

King of glo - ry! God him - self has come to save!
Long - a - wait - ed — once their hope, and now their King.
hearts in wor - ship! Let the King of glo - ry in!

We Adore You, Jesus Christ 3083
(Adoramus te Christe)

We a-dore you, Je - sus Christ, and we bless your ho - ly name;
A - do - ra - mus te Chris - te, be - ne - di - ci - mus ti - bi,

tru-ly your cross and pas - sion bring us life and heal - ing,
qui - a per cru - cem tu - am re - de - mi - sti mun-dum,

tru-ly your cross and pas - sion bring us life and heal - ing.
qui - a per cru - cem tu - am re - de - mi - sti mun-dum.

WORDS: Jacques Berthier
MUSIC: Jacques Berthier

ADORAMUS TE
77.76.76

3084 O Christ, You Hang upon a Cross

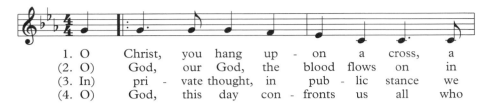

1. O   Christ,   you   hang   up - on   a   cross,   a
(2. O)   God,   our   God,   the   blood   flows   on   in
(3. In) pri - vate thought, in   pub - lic   stance   we
(4. O)   God,   this   day   con - fronts   us   all   who

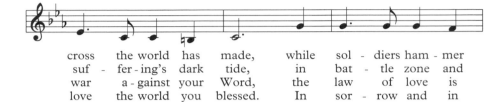

cross   the world   has   made,   while   sol - diers ham - mer
suf - fer - ing's   dark   tide,   in   bat - tle   zone   and
war   a - gainst   your   Word,   the   law   of   love   is
love   the world   you   blessed.   In   sor - row   and   in

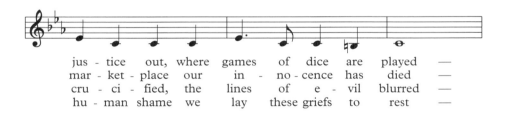

jus - tice   out, where   games   of   dice   are   played   —
mar - ket - place   our   in - no - cence   has   died   —
cru - ci - fied,   the   lines   of   e - vil   blurred   —
hu - man shame   we   lay   these griefs   to   rest   —

Chri - ste   e - le - i - son, Chri - ste   e - le - i - son.
Ky - ri - e   e - le - i - son, Ky-ri - e   e - le - i - son.
Chri - ste   e - le - i - son, Chri - ste   e - le - i - son.
Ky - ri - e   e - le - i - son, Ky-ri - e   e - le - i - son.

1-3 | 4

Chri - ste   e - le - i - son, Chri - ste   e - le - i - son. 2. O
Ky-ri - e   e - le - i - son, Ky-ri - e   e - le - i - son. 3. In
Chri - ste   e - le - i - son, Chri - ste   e - le - i - son. 4. O
Ky - ri - e   e - le - i - son, Ky-ri - e   e - le - i - son.

WORDS: Shirley Erena Murray
MUSIC: Colin Gibson

GOOD FRIDAY
86.86.66.66

The Power of the Cross

3085

1. Oh, to see the dawn of the dark-est day:
2. Oh, to see the pain writ-ten on your face,
3. Now the day-light flees; now the ground be-neath
4. Oh, to see my name writ-ten in the wounds,

Christ on the road to Cal-va-ry.
bear-ing the awe-some weight of sin.
quakes as its Mak-er bows his head.
for through your suf-fering I am free.

Tried by sin-ful men, torn and beat-en, then
Ev-ery bit-ter thought, ev-ery e-vil deed
Cur-tain torn in two, dead are raised to life.
Death is crushed to death, life is mine to live,

nailed to a cross of wood.
crown-ing your blood-stained brow.
"Fin-ished!" the vic-tory cry.
won through your self-less love!

Refrain

1-3. This the power of the cross; Christ be-came
4. This the power of the cross; Son of God

sin for us. Took the blame, bore the
slain for us. What a love, what a

| 1-3 | 4 | 4 |

wrath, we stand for-giv-en at the cross.
cost! We stand for-giv-en at the cross.

WORDS: Keith Getty and Stuart Townend
MUSIC: Keith Getty and Stuart Townend

POWER OF THE CROSS
10 8.10 8.12 14

3086 Day of Arising

1. Day of a - ris - ing, Christ on the road - way,
2. When we are walk - ing, doubt-ful and dread - ing,
3. "Lo, I am with you," Je - sus has spo - ken.
4. Christ our com - pan - ion, hope for the jour - ney,

un-known com - pan - ion walks with his own. _____
blind - ed by sad - ness, slow - ness of heart, _____
This is Christ's prom - ise, this is Christ's sign: _____
bread of com - pas - sion, o - pen our eyes. _____

When they in - vite him, as fades the first day,
yet Christ walks with us ev - er a - wait - ing
when the church gath - ers, when bread is bro - ken,
Grant us your vi - sion, set all hearts burn - ing

and bread is bro - ken, Christ is made known. ____
our in - vi - ta - tion: Stay, do not part. _____
there Christ is with us in bread and wine. _____
that all cre - a - tion with you may rise. _____

WORDS: Susan Palo Cherwien
MUSIC: Gaelic melody
Words © 1996 Susan Palo Cherwien; admin. Augsburg Fortress

BUNESSAN
55.54 D

3087 O Christ, When You Ascended

1. O Christ, when you as - cend - ed you took your right - ful
2. We look at earth - ly rul - ers and see what they com -
3. We're tempt - ed, Lord, to leave you in sto - ries nice - ly
4. It's of - ten quite a chal - lenge to fol - low in your
5. One day, O Lord, we'll know you, as we are ful - ly

WORDS: Carolyn Winfrey Gillette
MUSIC: Henry T. Smart
Words © 2007 Carolyn Winfrey Gillette

LANCASHIRE
76.76 D

throne;   your   time   on   earth   had   end - ed,   yet
mand: we   note   their   years   of   pow - er,   the
told;   some - times   we   don't   be - lieve   you   and
way;   we're   eas - i - ly   dis - tract - ed!   It's
known;   one   day   this   world   of   sin - ners   will

we   weren't   left   a - lone.   You   reign   o'er   earth   and
bor - ders   of   their   land.   Yet,   Lord,   you   are   not
say   your   ways   are   old.   Some - times   we   feel   so
hard,   Lord,   to   o - bey.   Some - times   we   give   you
bow   be - fore   your   throne.   One   day,   God's   whole   cre -

heav - en;   your   Spir - it   guides   our   way.   Your
bound - ed   by   things   like   time   and   space;   your
lone - ly   and   live   in   doubt   and   fear.   But
Sun - days,   an   ho - ur,   may - be   two.   But
a - tion   will   sing   and   praise   your   name;   on

prayers up - hold   your   peo - ple;   you   lead your church each   day.
reign   is   nev - er - end - ing,   you   rule   in   ev - ery   place.
your   as - cen - sion means,   Lord, you're   pres - ent   with   us   here.
your   as - cen - sion means,   Lord,   all   life   be - longs   to   you.
earth   as   now   in   heav - en,   we'll   cel - e - brate   your   reign.

3088

Easter Alleluia

Refrain   *Fine*

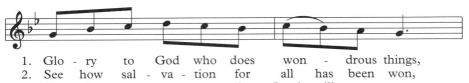

Al-le-lu-ia,   al-le-lu-ia,   al-le-lu - ia! _____

1. Glo - ry to God who does won - drous things,
2. See how sal - va - tion for all has been won,
3. Now in our pres - ence the Lord will ap - pear,
4. Call us, Good Shep - herd, we lis - ten for you,
5. Lord, we are o - pen to all that you say,
6. If we have love, then we dwell in the Lord,

let all the peo - ple God's prais - es now sing,
up from the grave our new life has be - gun,
shine in the fa - ces of all of us here,
want - ing to see you in all that we do,
read - y to lis - ten and fol - low your way,
God will pro - tect us from fire and sword,

all of cre - a - tion in splen - dor shall ring:
life now per - fect - ed in Je - sus the Son:
fill us with joy and cast out all our fear:
we would the gate of sal - va - tion pass through:
you are the pot - ter and we are the clay:
fill us with love and the peace of his word:

                                                      D.C.

Al - le - lu - ia! _____

WORDS: Marty Haugen
MUSIC: 15th cent. French carol; adapt. by Marty Haugen
Words and adapt. © 1986 GIA Publications, Inc.

O FILII ET FILIAE
10 10 10 with Alleluias

O Living God

3089

1. O liv-ing God, I long to see you lift-ed
2. O liv-ing God, I long to praise you heart and
3. O liv-ing God, I soon will see you face to

up in all your glo-ry; to
voice, with all cre-a-tion; to
face, in all your glo-ry. I'll

see you there in ho-ly beau-ty. O
wor-ship you for ten-der mer-cy. O
wor-ship you in end-less won-der. O

Lord, al-might-y God, liv-ing Christ, I love you.
Lord, al-might-y God, liv-ing Christ, I love you.
Lord, al-might-y God, liv-ing Christ, I love you.

WORDS: Ken Bible
MUSIC: Traditional USA folk tune; arr. by Ken Bible

SHENANDOAH
989.66

3090

The Easter Song

1. Hear the bells ring - ing, they're sing - ing that
2. Hear the bells ring - ing, they're sing - ing, "Christ

we can be born a - gain!
is ris - en from the dead!"

The an - gel up - on the tomb-stone said,

"He is ris - en just as he said. Quick - ly

WORDS: Anne Herring
MUSIC: Anne Herring

EASTER SONG
Irr.

3091

Come, Holy Spirit

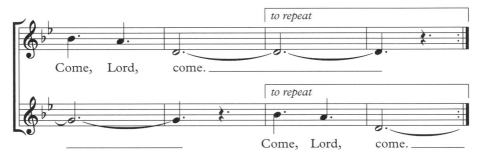

*Maranatha means "Come, soon."

WORDS: The Iona Community
MUSIC: The Iona Community

IONA MARANATHA
55.43

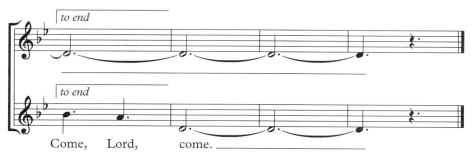

Come, Lord, come.

Come, Holy Spirit — 3092

Refrain

Come, Ho - ly Spir - it, O how we need you.

Come, Ho - ly Spir - it, we need you.

1. Come with grace and fire. Might-y rush-ing wind,
2. Come with heav-en's power, let the rains des - cend,

Com - fort - er and Breath of Heav - en, fill my heart a -
times of sweet re - fresh - ing. Je - sus,

gain. fill my heart, heal my heart, fill my heart,

heal my heart, fill my heart a - gain.

WORDS: Israel Houghton
MUSIC: Israel Houghton

COME, HOLY SPIRIT
Irr.

3093

Fill My Cup, Lord

1. Like the wom-an at the well I was seek-ing for
2. There are mil-lions in this world who are crav-ing the
3. So, my neigh-bor, if the things this world gave you leave

things that could not sat-is-fy; and then I heard my Sav-ior
pleas-ure earth-ly things af-ford; but none can match the won-drous
hun-gers that won't pass a-way, my bless-ed Lord will come and

speak-ing: "Draw from my well that nev-er shall run dry."
treas-ure that I find in Je-sus Christ my Lord.
save you, if you kneel to him and hum-bly pray:

Refrain

Fill my cup, Lord, I lift it up, Lord! Come and

WORDS: Richard Blanchard
MUSIC: Richard Blanchard
© 1964 Word Music, LLC

FILL MY CUP
Irr. with Refrain

quench this thirst-ing of my soul; bread of heav-en, feed me 'til I

want no more — fill my cup, fill it up and make me whole!

Come to Me 3094

Come to me, come to me, weak and heav-y lad-en; ___
lad-en, lad-en;

lad - en; ___

trust in me, lean on me. I will give you rest. ____

WORDS: Paraphrased from Matthew 11:28
MUSIC: John L. Bell

COME TO ME
66.65

3095 Somebody's Knockin' at Your Door

Refrain

Some-bod - y's knock-in' at your door; some-bod - y's

knock-in' at your door; O sin - ner, why don't you

an - swer? Some-bod - y's knock-in' at your door. _____

Leader   *All*

1. Knocks like Je - sus.
2. Can't you hear him?   Some-bod - y's knock-in' at your door.
3. Je - sus calls you.
4. Can't you trust him?

WORDS: African American spiritual   SOMEBODY'S KNOCKIN'
MUSIC: African American spiritual, harm. by Richard Proulx   Irr.

Harm. © 1986 GIA Publications, Inc.

3096

Gentle Shepherd

WORDS: Gloria Gaither
MUSIC: William J. Gaither

GENTLE SHEPHERD
Irr.

day;_____ gen-tle Shep-herd,___ come and lead us,___

___ for we need you to help us find our way.___

Depth of Mercy 3097

1. Depth of mer-cy! Can there be mer-cy still re-served for
2. I have long with-stood his grace, long pro-voked him to his
3. I my Mas-ter have de-nied, I a-fresh have cru-ci-
4. There for me the Sav-ior stands, shows his wounds and spreads his
5. Now in-cline me to re-pent, let me now my sins la-

me? Can my God his wrath for-bear, me, the
face, would not heark-en to his calls, grieved him
fied, oft pro-faned his hal-lowed name, put him
hands. God is love! I know, I feel; Je-sus
ment, now my foul re-volt de-plore, weep, be-

chief of sin-ners spare, me, the chief of sin-ners spare?
by a thou-sand falls, grieved him by a thou-sand falls.
to an o-pen shame, put him to an o-pen shame.
weeps and loves me still, Je-sus weeps and loves me still.
lieve, and sin no more, weep, be-lieve, and sin no more.

WORDS: Charles Wesley
MUSIC: Penny Rodriguez

GOTTES ZEIT
77.77

Music © 2005 Abingdon Press, admin. by The Copyright Company

3098

Dust and Ashes

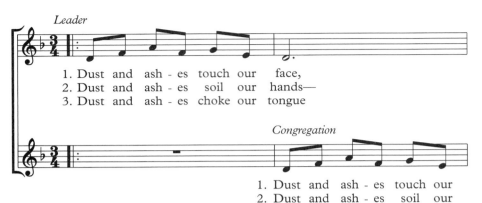

1. Dust and ash - es touch our face,
2. Dust and ash - es soil our hands—
3. Dust and ash - es choke our tongue

Congregation

1. Dust and ash - es touch our
2. Dust and ash - es soil our
3. Dust and ash - es choke our

mark our fail - ure and our fall - ing.
greed of mar - ket, pride of na - tion.
in the waste-land of de - pres - sion.

face,
hands—
tongue

mark our fail - ure and our
greed of mar - ket, pride of
in the waste-land of de -

Ho - ly Spir - it, come, walk with us to - mor - row,
Ho - ly Spir - it, come, walk with us to - mor - row,
Ho - ly Spir - it, come, walk with us to - mor - row,

fall - ing.
na - tion.
pres - sion.

WORDS: Brian Wren
MUSIC: David Haas

DUST AND ASHES
7 8.11 14 with Refrain

3099 Falling on My Knees

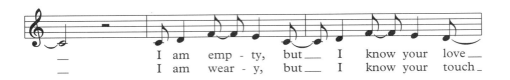

1. Hun-gry, I come to ___ you, for I know _ you sat - is - fy. ___
2. Bro-ken, I run to ___ you, for your arms _ are o - pen wide; ___

___ I am emp - ty, but ___ I know your love ___
___ I am wear - y, but ___ I know your touch ___

Refrain

___ does not run dry. ___ So I wait for you. ___
___ re - stores my life. ___

___ So I wait for you. ___ I'm fall - ing on my knees, ___

___ of - fer - ing all of me. ___ Je - sus, ___

___ you're all this heart _ is liv - ing for. ___

WORDS: Kathryn Scott
MUSIC: Kathryn Scott

FALLING ON MY KNEES
67.94 with Refrain

Jesus Paid It All

1. I hear the Sav-ior say, "Thy strength in-deed is small.
2. Lord, now in-deed I find thy power, and thine a-lone
3. For noth-ing good have I where-by thy grace to claim;
4. And when, be-fore the throne, I stand in him com-plete,

Child of weak-ness, watch and pray, find in me thine all in all."
Can change the lep-er's spots and melt the heart of stone.
I'll wash my gar-ments clean in the blood of Cal-vary's Lamb.
"Je-sus died my soul to save," my lips shall still re-peat.

Refrain

Je - sus paid it all, all to him I owe;

sin had left a crim-son stain, he washed it white as snow.

WORDS: Elvina M. Hall
MUSIC: John T. Grape

ALL TO CHRIST
66.77 with Refrain

3101

Love Lifted Me

1. I was sink-ing deep in sin, far from the peace-ful shore,
2. Souls in dan-ger, look a-bove, Je - sus com-plete-ly saves;

ver - y deep - ly stained with-in, sink-ing to rise no more;
he will lift you by his love out of the an - gry waves.

but the Mas - ter of the sea heard my de-spair-ing cry,
He's the Mas - ter of the sea, bil - lows his will o - bey;

from the wa - ters lift - ed me; now safe am I.
he your Sav - ior wants to be — be saved to - day.

WORDS: James Rowe
MUSIC: Howard E. Smith

LOVE LIFTED ME
76.74 with Refrain

Refrain

Love lift - ed e - ven me! Love lift - ed e - ven me!

When noth - ing else could help. Love lift - ed me.

Love lift - ed e - ven me! Love lift - ed e - ven me!

When noth - ing else could help. Love lift - ed me.

3102

You Are My King

WORDS: Billy James Foote
MUSIC: Billy James Foote

AMAZING LOVE
Irr. with Refrain

D.S. al Coda

CODA

King! You are my___ King!

And it's my joy to hon - or you. __ In all I___

__ do I hon - or you. __ In all I___

__ do I hon - or you. __

Purify My Heart   3103

1. Pur - i - fy my heart, O Fa - ther;
2. Turn my heart a - way from an - ger;
3. Turn my heart toward those who love me;
4. Turn my heart toward truth, O Fa - ther;
5. Turn my heart toward you, O Fa - ther;

pur - i - fy my heart, O Je - sus; pur - i - fy my heart, O
turn my heart a - way from en - vy; turn my heart a - way from
turn my heart toward an - y neigh-bor; turn my heart toward foe and
turn my heart toward life, O Je - sus; turn my heart toward joy, O
turn my heart toward you, O Je - sus; turn my heart toward you, O

Spir - it; I want to see my God.
fol - ly; O pur - i - fy my heart.
stran - ger; I want to see my God.
Spir - it; O pur - i - fy my heart.
Spir - it; I want to see my God.

WORDS: Richard Leach
MUSIC: Amanda Husberg

TURN MY HEART
88.86

3104

Amazing Grace
(My Chains Are Gone)

1. A - maz - ing grace! how sweet the sound that
(2. 'Twas) grace that taught my heart to fear; and
(3. The) Lord has prom - ised good to me; his
(4. The) earth shall soon dis - solve like snow, the

saved a wretch like me! I once was lost but
grace my fears re - lieved. How pre - cious did that
word my hope se - cures. He will my shield and
sun for - bear to shine. But God who called me

Last time to Coda |1

now am found; was blind, but now I see. 2. 'Twas
grace ap - pear the hour I first be -
por - tion be as long as life en -
here be - low, will be for - ev - er

|2, 3| *Refrain*

lieved.
dures. My chains are gone, I've been set ____ free. My God, my

Sav - ior, has ran - somed me. And like a flood his mer - cy

|1 |2

reigns, un - end - ing love, a - maz - ing grace.

|2   *D.S.*|3

3. The grace. My chains are grace. 4. The

CODA

mine, will be for - ev - er mine. You are for - ev - er mine.

WORDS: John Newton (sts.), refrain by Chris Tomlin, and Louie Giglio   MY CHAINS ARE GONE
MUSIC: Traditional American melody; refrain and arr. by Chris Tomlin and Louis Giglio   Irr.

In Christ Alone

1. In Christ a-lone my hope is found, he is my
2. In Christ a-lone, who took on flesh, full-ness of
3. There in the ground his bod-y lay, Light of the
4. No guilt in life, no fear in death, this is the

light, my strength, my song. This Cor-ner-stone, this sol-id
God in help-less babe. This gift of love and righ-teous-
world by dark-ness slain. Then burst-ing forth in glo-rious
power of Christ in me. From life's first cry to fi-nal

ground, firm through the fierc-est drought and
ness scorned by the ones he came to
day, up from the grave he rose a-
breath, Je-sus com-mands my des-ti-

storm. What heights of love, what depths of peace, when fears are
save. 'Til on that cross as Je-sus died the wrath of
gain! And as he stands in vic-to-ry, sin's curse has
ny. No power of hell, no scheme or plan can ev-er

stilled, when striv-ings cease! My Com-fort-er, my all in
God was sat-is-fied; for ev-ery sin on him was
lost its grip on me. For I am his and he is
pluck me from his hand. 'Til he re-turns or calls me

all, here in the love of Christ I stand.
laid. Here in the death of Christ I live.
mine, bought with the pre-cious blood of Christ.
home, here in the power of Christ I'll stand.

WORDS: Keith Getty and Stuart Townend
MUSIC: Keith Getty and Stuart Townend

IN CHRIST ALONE
LMD

3106

Your Grace Is Enough

1. Great is your faith-ful-ness, O God. _
2. Great is your love _ and jus - tice, God. _

You wres-tle with _ the sin-ner's heart. _
You use the weak _ to lead the strong. _

You lead us by _ still wa - ters in - to mer - cy.
You lead us in _ the song of your _ sal - va - tion,

and noth-ing can _ keep us a - part. _
and all your peo - ple sing a - long. _ So re -

mem - ber your peo - ple, re - mem - ber your chil - dren, re -

mem - ber your prom - ise, O God. _ Your

Refrain

grace is e - nough, _ your grace is e - nough _ your

WORDS: Matt Maher
MUSIC: Matt Maher

YOUR GRACE IS ENOUGH
Irr.

Last time to Coda

grace is e-nough __ for me. __ Your

grace is e-nough, __ your grace is e-nough, __ your

grace is e-nough __ for me. __ So re-

CODA

grace is e-nough. __ Heav-en reach-ing down to us. __ Your

grace is e-nough __ for me. __ God, __ I see your

grace is e-nough. __ I'm cov-ered in your love. __ Your

grace is e-nough __ for me, __ for me. __

Sing first time only

3

3107 Just a Little Talk with Jesus

1. I once was lost in sin but Jesus took me in,
2. Some-times my path seems drear, with-out a ray of cheer,
3. I may have doubts and fears, my eyes be filled with tears,

and then a lit-tle light from heav-en filled my soul;
and then a cloud of doubt may hide the light of day;
but Je-sus is a friend who watch-es day and night;

it bathed my heart in love and wrote my name a-bove,
the mists of sin may rise and hide the star-ry skies,
I go to him in prayer, he knows my ev-ery care,

Refrain

and just a lit-tle talk with Je-sus made me whole.
but just a lit-tle talk with Je-sus clears the way.
and just a lit-tle talk with Je-sus makes it right.

Now let us

WORDS: Cleavant Derricks
MUSIC: Cleavant Derricks
© 1937 Bridge Building (BMI)

JUST A LITTLE TALK
6 6 12 D with Refrain

3108 Tradin' My Sorrows

I'm trad-in' my __ sor-rows, I'm trad-in' my __ shame, I'm lay-in' them down for the joy of the Lord. I'm trad-in' my __ sick-ness, I'm trad-in' my __ pain, I'm lay-in' them down for the joy of the Lord. Yes, Lord, yes, Lord, yes, yes, Lord. Yes, Lord, yes, Lord, yes, yes, Lord.

Last time to Coda

Yes, Lord, yes, Lord, yes, yes, Lord. A-men. __ I am pressed __ but not crushed, per-se-cut-ed, not a-ban-doned; struck down but not de-

WORDS: Darrell Evans
MUSIC: Darrell Evans

TRADIN' MY SORROWS
Irr.

© 1998, arr. © 2010 Integrity's Hosanna! Music (ASCAP) c/o Integrity Media, Inc., admin. at EMICMGPublishing.com

stroyed. I am blessed beyond the curse, for his

prom-ise will en-dure that his joy's gon-na be my strength.

Though the sor - row may

D.S. al Coda

last for the night, his joy comes with the morn - in'.

CODA

Yes, Lord, yes, Lord, yes, yes, Lord. A - men.

Living Spirit, Holy Fire 3109

1. Liv - ing Spir - it, ho - ly fire, burn-ing bright to light our
2. Warm us, draw your peo - ple near when our love draws weak or
3. Melt a - way the masks we wear, hid - ing what we know and
4. O - pen hearts; af - firm us all, man - y - splen-dored, one in

way, blaze a - mong us and in - spire lives that
cold. Free our fro - zen hearts from fear, that each
feel. Risk-ing growth, we want to share love in
you, we em - brace the work, the call: you are

praise you day by day.
sto - ry may be told.
ac - tion, love that's real.
mak - ing all things new.

WORDS: Ruth Duck
MUSIC: Lori True
Words © 2005, music © 2007 GIA Publications, Inc.

ALL THINGS NEW
77.77

3110   By Grace We Have Been Saved

1. By grace we have been saved through faith and
2. For all have sinned and fall - en short. God's
3. God gave to earth a per - fect love through
4. We know the wage of sin is death; thank
5. Set free, we now have peace with God. Sal -

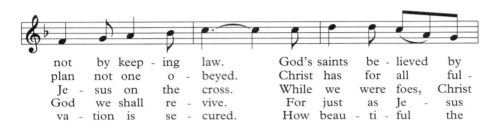

not by keep - ing law. God's saints be - lieved by
plan not one o - beyed. Christ has for all ful -
Je - sus on the cross. While we were foes, Christ
God we shall re - vive. For just as Je - sus
va - tion is se - cured. How beau - ti - ful the

what they heard and not by what they
filled the law. Be - lieve, con - fess, be
died for us. We gained by God's own
rose a - gain, we too are made a -
feet of those who share the gos - pel

saw, and not by what they saw.
saved; be - lieve, con - fess, be saved.
loss, we gained by God's own loss.
live, we too are made a - live.
word, who share the gos - pel word.

WORDS: Rusty Edwards

MUSIC: *The Southern Harmony*

DOVE OF PEACE

CM

Redemption

Refrain

Lord, re-deem our bro-ken world. Lord, re-deem our bro-ken world.

1, 2, 3 *to Verses*
Leader
4
Fine

1. De - world.
2. __
3. __

Leader(s) (opt.)

(1.) liv - er us from fear____ and sad - ness, hope-
2. Res - cue us from pride__ and an - ger, self -
3. Send us your a - noin - ted one to heal _

less - ness and pain;__ __ save us from our a -
ish - ness and greed;_ __ give us hope and give -
__ and make us whole,_ to break the bonds of sin__

D.C.

pa - thy, our bro - ken - ness, our shame. _
__ us life. Re - store_ us, set us free.____
__ and death to lift____ our wear - y souls.__

The choral parts may be sung softly underneath the Leader parts.
**Optional harmony (upper notes) on stanzas 2 and 3.*

WORDS: Josh Tinley
MUSIC: Josh Tinley
© 2008 Josh Tinley

REDEMPTION
Irr. with Refrain

3112

Breathe

WORDS: Marie Barnett
MUSIC: Marie Barnett

BREATHE
Irr. with Refrain

CODA

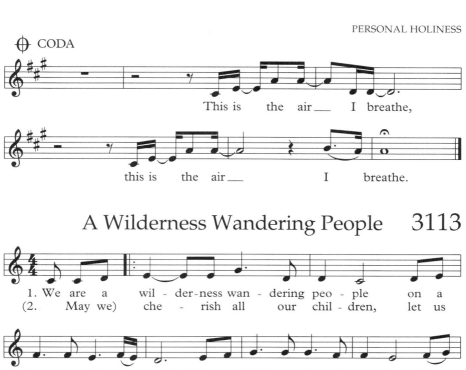

This is the air ___ I breathe,

this is the air ___ I breathe.

A Wilderness Wandering People   3113

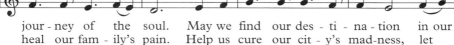

1. We are a wil - der-ness wan - dering peo - ple on a
(2. May we) che - rish all our chil - dren, let us

jour - ney of the soul. May we find our des - ti - na - tion in our
heal our fam - ily's pain. Help us cure our cit - y's mad-ness, let

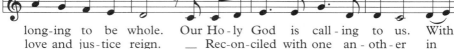

long-ing to be whole. Our Ho - ly God is call - ing to us. With
love and jus-tice reign. ___ Rec-on-ciled with one an - oth-er in

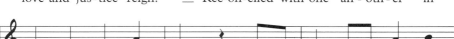

Je - sus by our side may com - pas - sion be our
prayer and praise and song, we're the bod - y of Christ to -

1

com - pass; may the Spir - it be our guide. _____ 2. May we
geth - er and we know that we be -

2

long, we be - long, _____ we be - long, _____ we be-long.

WORDS: Jim Strathdee
MUSIC: Jim Strathdee
© 1996 Desert Flower Music

WILDERNESS
Irr.

3114

Come to the Water

1. There's a war going on just across the street, there's a
(2. There's a) cry from the child in the fac-to-ry, there's a

rage that's burn-ing to an an-gry beat.
prayer for the pris-on-ers of pov-er-ty.

I can feel the thirst but there's no re-lief. We need a
Save us from the greed and the ap-a-thy. We need a

riv-er.
riv-er.
There's a sound in the dis-tance like a
There's a hope like a flood run-ning

thun-der cloud, we're wait-ing for the rain while the
down our street, we're an ar-my of peace-mak-ers

sun beats down. Can you feel it ris-ing from the
on our feet. Take us to the place love and

un-der-ground? We need a riv-er.
mer-cy meet. There is a riv-er.

WORDS: Paul Baloche, Steven Curtis-Chapman, Stuart Garrard, Israel Houghton,
   Tim Hughes, Graham Kendrick, Andy Park, Matt Redman, Martin Smith,
   Michael W. Smith, Chris Tomlin, and Darlene Zschech
MUSIC: Paul Baloche, Steven Curtis-Chapman, Stuart Garrard, Israel Houghton,
   Tim Hughes, Graham Kendrick, Andy Park, Matt Redman, Martin Smith,
   Michael W. Smith, Chris Tomlin, and Darlene Zschech

COME TO THE WATER
Irr.

3115

Covenant Prayer

Lord, I am not mine, but yours a - lone. _ Let your will be
Spir - it hear my cry, for - ev - er I am

done and not my own. _ Put me where you
yours and you are mine. _ Fa - ther, Son and

will, and let me serve; in ev - ery-thing I
Spir - it hear my cry, for - ev - er I am

Refrain

do, let me en - dure. _ This is my
yours and you are mine. _

prayer, Lord, to you. _ My prom - ise and my

vow, strong and true. _ And the cov - en - ant I make _

_ on earth, let it be ful - filled in

WORDS: John Wesley
MUSIC: Jay D. Locklear and Adam Seate

COVENANT
Irr.

3116 Love the Lord

1. Love the Lord, your God with all your heart, __
2. I will serve the Lord with all my heart, __

__ with all your soul, with all your mind, __
__ with all my soul, with all my mind, __

__ and with all your strength. __
__ and with all my strength. __

Love the Lord, your God with all your heart, __
I will serve the Lord with all my heart, __

__ with all your soul, with all your mind, __
__ with all my soul, with all my mind, __

__ and with all your strength. __ With all your heart, __
__ and with all my strength. __ With all my heart, __

__ with all your soul, __ with all your mind, __
__ with all my soul, __ with all my mind, __
(D.S.) __ with all my soul, __ with all my mind, __

WORDS: Lincoln Brewster
MUSIC: Lincoln Brewster

LOVE THE LORD
Irr.

3117   Rule of Life

Do all the good you can, _____ by all the
means you can, _____ in all the ways you can, _____
_____ in all the plac-es you can, _____ at all the
times you can, _____ to all the peo-ple you can, _____ as long as
ev - er _____ you can. _____

WORDS: 18th cent. aphorism, attr. to John Wesley
MUSIC: Edward Bonnemere

© Amity Music

RULE OF LIFE
Irr.

3118   Take This Moment, Sign, and Space

1. Take this mo - ment, sign, and space; take my
2. Take the time to call my name, take the
3. Take the tired - ness of my days, take my
4. Take the lit - tle child in me, scared of
5. Take my tal - ents, take my skills, take what's

WORDS: John L. Bell
MUSIC: John L. Bell and Graham Maule

© 1989 Wild Goose Resource Group, The Iona Community, admin. by GIA Publications, Inc.

TAKE THIS MOMENT
75.75

friends a - round;____ here a - mong us
time to mend____ who I am and
past re - gret,____ let - ting your for -
grow - ing old;____ help me here to
yet to be;____ let my life be

make the place where your love is found.___
what I've been, all I've failed to tend.___
give - ness touch all I can't for - get.___
find my worth made in Christ's own mold.___
yours, and yet, let it still be me.___

Take, O Take Me As I Am

3119

Take, O take me as I am; sum-mon out what I shall

be; set your seal up-on my heart and live in me.

WORDS: John L. Bell
MUSIC: John L. Bell

TAKE, O TAKE
7 7 11

3120 Amazing Abundance

1. A - maz - ing a - bun - dance poured out on this
2. A ho - ly com - pas - sion is born through the
3. We pray for com - mun - ion, all na - tions so

land, _____ the mark of your gra - cious and gen - er - ous
cries _____ when trag - e - dy threat - ens and he - roes a -
strong _____ that dif-ference is hon - ored and all might be -

hand. _____ Your bless-ing is rich - est on those who will
rise. _____ God's spir - it is pres - ent and felt ev - ery -
long. _____ A tap - es - try wov - en by myr - i - ad

give _____ with joy and thanks - giv - ing so
where _____ that hands reach through dark - ness and
hands, _____ a ban - ner of free - dom the

1, 2   3   3   Refrain

oth - ers may live.   2. A
bat - tle des - pair.   3. We
bright braid-ed   strands.   Praise

God for the na - tions, O help us to see _____ the

whole world is yours, Lord, and yearns to be free! _____

WORDS: Laurie Zelman
MUSIC: Mark A. Miller

ABUNDANCE
65.65 D with Refrain

© 2003 Abingdon Press, admin. by The Copyright Company

If You Believe and I Believe

If you be-lieve and I be-lieve and we to-geth-er pray,

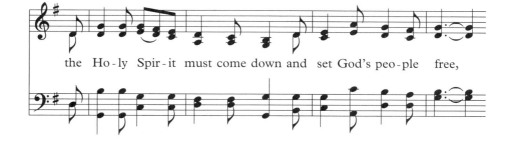

the Ho-ly Spir-it must come down and set God's peo-ple free,

and set God's peo-ple free, and set God's peo-ple free;

the Ho-ly Spir-it must come down and set God's peo-ple free.

WORDS: Traditional Zimbabwe
MUSIC: Traditional Zimbabwe, arr. by John L. Bell

IF YOU BELIEVE
Irr.

3122   Christ Has Broken Down the Wall

1. Christ has bro-ken down the wall,
2. We're ac-cept-ed as we are,
3. Cast a-side your doubts and fears,
4. We will tear down the walls!

Christ has bro-ken down the wall.   Let us join our
we're ac-cept-ed as we are.   Through God's love all is
cast a-side your doubts and fears.   Peace and love, free-ly
We will tear down ev-ery wall!   God has called us,

[1-4]

hearts as one,   Christ has bro-ken down the wall.
rec-on-ciled,   we're ac-cept-ed as we are.
of-fered here;   cast a-side your doubts and fears.
one and all;   Christ has bro-ken down the wall!

Optional ending

wall!   Christ has bro-ken down the wall!

WORDS: Mark A. Miller
MUSIC: Mark A. Miller
© 2011 Choristers Guild

BROKEN WALLS
Irr.

3123   Here Is Peace

1. Here is peace, when grace a-stounds us, quell-ing
2. Here is peace, when grace en-gen-ders love that
3. Here is peace, when grace sur-pris-es ig-no-

all our wild pre-tense.   Here is peace, sha-lom and
nei-ther fades nor ends.   Here is peace when peo-ple
rance with words of hope.   Here is peace to light our

WORDS: Andrew Pratt
MUSIC: Traditional Latvian melody

HERE IS PEACE
87.87

Words © 2010 Stainer & Bell Ltd., admin. by Hope Publishing Company

kind - ness, pas - sion ruled by rea - soned sense.
wel - come; en - e - mies be - come as friends.
sens - es; see, God's love has bound-less scope.

How Shall I Come Before the Lord   3124

1. How shall I come be - fore the Lord and bow my-
2. Will fin - est gifts bring God's de - light? Will wealth bring
3. Let jus-tice shine in all your ways. Let lov - ing

self with heart out - poured? And shall I come with of - fer-
fa - vor in God's sight? What must we be? What must we
kind - ness rule your days, that, as this earth - ly path you

ing? What shall I give? What shall I bring?
do? What does the Lord re - quire of you?
trod, you shall walk hum - bly with your God.

WORDS: Dean McIntyre
MUSIC: English folk melody; harm. by Dean McIntyre

O WALY WALY
LM

Words and harm. © 2005 The General Board of Discipleship of The United Methodist Church

3125   Peace for the Children

1. Peace for the chil-dren, peace, peace. Peace for the chil-dren we
2. Peace for the wom-en, peace, peace. Peace for the wom-en we
3. Peace for the men, peace, peace. Peace for the men we
4. Peace in our fam-i-lies, peace, peace. Peace in our fam-ilies we
5. Peace for the na-tions, peace, peace. Peace for the na-tions we

pray.   Fol-low-ing the path of One of peace, we
pray.   Fol-low-ing the path of One of peace, we
pray.   Fol-low-ing the path of One of peace, we
pray.   Fol-low-ing the path of One of peace, we
pray.   Fol-low-ing the path of One of peace, we

work for heal-ing, we work for peace; peace for the chil-dren to-day.
work for heal-ing, we work for peace; peace for the wom-en to-day.
work for heal-ing, we work for peace; peace for the men to-day.
work for heal-ing, we work for peace; peace for our fam-ilies to-day.
work for heal-ing, we work for peace; peace for the na-tions to-day.

6. Peace for the creatures...
7. Peace for our planet...
8. Peace in the universe...

9. *Hum this verse softly, during which time individuals may call out the word "peace" in other languages, making a global connection.*
10. Peace in the soul...

WORDS: Doreen Lankshear-Smith
MUSIC: Doreen Lankshear-Smith

PEACE FOR ALL
Irr.

© 1993 Doreen Lankshear-Smith

3126   Everything That Has Voice

1. Ev-ery-thing that has voice, sing for peace, speak for peace,
2. All the world longs for peace, cries for peace, dies for peace;
3. Ev-ery-one who has breath, you and I, pass-ers-by,

giv-en chance, giv-en choice, work for peace, write for peace,
let the chil-dren, ev-ery place, sleep in peace, grow in peace,
ev-ery ten-ant of the earth, plant for peace, gath-er peace,

WORDS: Shirley Erena Murray
MUSIC: Marty Haugen

SING FOR PEACE
66.76.779

Words © 2004 Hope Publishing Company; music © 2005 GIA Publications, Inc.

res - o - nat - ing ev - ery - where,   ech - o - ing our com - mon
home and coun-try safe to   be   where the Spir - it ris - es
cul - ti - vate a neigh-bor - hood   cher - ish - ing our neigh-bor's

care: ev-ery-thing   that has voice   sing for   peace!___
free: all the world   longs for peace   cries for   peace.___
good: ev-ery - one   who has breath   live in   peace.___

I Have a Dream   3127

1. "I   have   a   dream," a   man   once said, "where
2. But   in   this   world   of   bit - ter strife   the
3. Fierce   per - se - cu - tion,   war,   and hate   are
4. So   dream   the   dreams   and   sing   the songs,   but
5. Lord,   give   us   vi - sion,   make   us strong,   help

all   is   per - fect   peace;   where   men   and wom - en,
dream can   of - ten   fade;   re - al - i - ty   seems
rag - ing   ev - ery - where;   God   calls   us   now   to
nev - er   be   con - tent;   for   thoughts and words don't
us   to   do   your   will;   don't   let   us   rest   un -

black and white, stand   hand   in   hand, and   all u - nite in
dark as   night, we   catch   but glimps - es   of the light Christ
pay   the price through strug - gles   and through sac - ri - fice of
ease   the pain: un - less there's ac - tion,   all is   vain; faith
til   we   see   your   love through-out   hu - man - i - ty   u -

free - dom   and   in   love,   in   free - dom and   in   love."
sheds on   hu - man - kind,   Christ sheds on   hu - man-kind.
stand - ing   for   the   right,   of   stand - ing for   the right.
proves it - self   in   deeds,   faith proves it - self   in deeds.
nit - ing   us   in   peace,   u - nit - ing us   in peace.

WORDS: Pamela J. Pettitt   REPTON
MUSIC: Charles Hubert Hastings Parry   86.886
Words © Pam Pettitt

3128

Whatever You Do

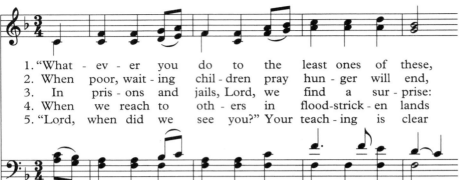

1. "What - ev - er you do to the least ones of these,
2. When poor, wait - ing chil - dren pray hun - ger will end,
3. In pris - ons and jails, Lord, we find a sur - prise:
4. When we reach to oth - ers in flood-strick - en lands
5. "Lord, when did we see you?" Your teach - ing is clear

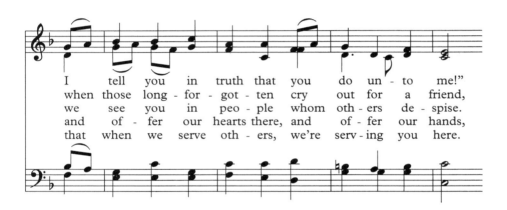

I tell you in truth that you do un - to me!"
when those long - for - got - ten cry out for a friend,
we see you in peo - ple whom oth - ers de - spise.
and of - fer our hearts there, and of - fer our hands,
that when we serve oth - ers, we're serv - ing you here.

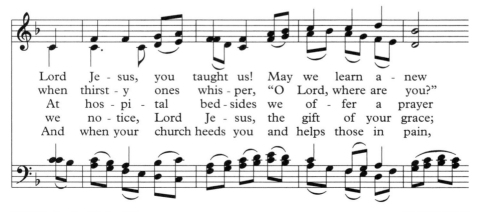

Lord Je - sus, you taught us! May we learn a - new
when thirst - y ones whis - per, "O Lord, where are you?"
At hos - pi - tal bed - sides we of - fer a prayer
we no - tice, Lord Je - sus, the gift of your grace;
And when your church heeds you and helps those in pain,

WORDS: Carolyn Winfrey Gillette
MUSIC: William J. Kirkpatrick; arr. by David Willcocks

CRADLE SONG
11 11.11 11

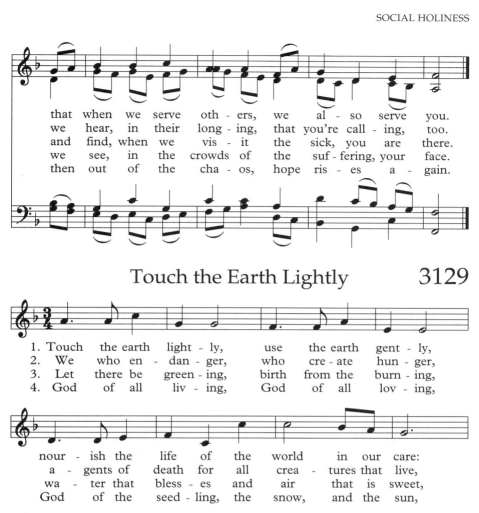

Touch the Earth Lightly   3129

WORDS: Shirley Erena Murray
MUSIC: Swee-Hong Lim

AI HU
10 10.10 10

3130

Come, Emmanuel

1., 4. Come and speak to us, come and re-new us, come and live
2. Once mer-cy found us, still you a-stound us, hold and sur-
3. Love that be-gins us, par-dons and wins us, come and reign

through us, Em-man-u-el. _____ Grace to im-plore us,
round us, Em-man-u-el. _____ Liv-ing in-side us,
in us, Em-man-u-el. _____ Come and speak to us,

Last time to Coda

ev-er be-fore us, come and re-store us, Em-man-u-
faith-ful to guide us, cov-er and hide us, Em-man-u-
fill and re-new us, come and live through us, Em-man-u-

Refrain

el. _____ Come, _____ Em-man-u-el; _____
el. _____

_ come, _____ Em-man-u-el. _____

Come, _____ Em-man-u-el; _____ come, _____

3   **1, 2**   **3**   *D.C.*

_ Em-man-u-el. _____

Coda

el, _____ Em-man-u-el, Em-man-u-el. _____

WORDS: Twila Paris
MUSIC: Twila Paris

COME EMMANUEL
10 9.10 9 with Refrain

Hear My Prayer, O God

3131

1. Hear my prayer, O God, and lis - ten to my plea;
2. Hound - ed by a foe who crushed me to the ground,
3. An - swer soon, O God, my spir - it faints in me;
4. Keep me safe, O God, and help me learn your will;

faith - ful, right - eous One, give ear and an - swer me.
I am like the dead or those in pris - on bound.
do not hide your face, or I will cease to be.
let your Spir - it lead through lev - el path - ways still.

Judge me not, I pray; no mer - it dare I claim;
Hope - less, numbed by fear, I pon - der all your care;
When the morn - ing dawns, make known your love a - new;
For your great Name's sake, my griefs and fears dis - pel;

know - ing my own faults, I trust in your just Name.
thirs - ty as parched earth, I lift my hands in prayer.
show me how to walk, for I will trust in you.
free me from my foes, that I may serve you well.

WORDS: Carl P. Daw, Jr., based on Psalm 143
MUSIC: Hal H. Hopson

HYMN CHANT
56.56 D

3132 House of God

1. This is the house of God. This is the gate of heav-en.
2. Live in the house of God. Live at the gate of heav-en.
3. You are the house of God. You are the gate of heav-en.

This is a ho-ly place. You are al-ways wel-come.
Live in a ho-ly place. You are al-ways wel-come.
You are a ho-ly place. I am al-ways wel-come.

Trust and know I'm al-ways with you through all chan-ges
You are al-ways pre-cious to me. You are al-ways
Through your tears and through your cour-age, through all tri-als

and all sea-sons. When you wake and when you're sleep-ing.
per-fect to me. Stop your wor-ry, your ex-cus-es.
and all sto-ries. Cra-dled in my arms please hear me.

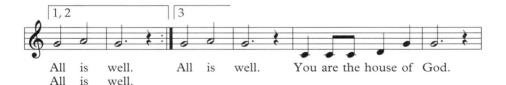

| 1, 2 | | 3 |

All is well. All is well. You are the house of God.
All is well.

You are the gate of heav-en. You are a ho-ly place.

I am al-ways wel-come. This is the house of God.

WORDS: Mariénne Kreitlow HOUSE OF GOD
MUSIC: Mariénne Kreitlow 67.66.88.83

Kyrie

3133

Ky-ri - e   e - le - i - son.   Chris-te   e - le - i - son.

Ky-ri - e   e - le - i - son.   Grant to us your peace,   Lord. _____

MUSIC: Steve Garnaas-Holmes

Music © 1990 Steve Garnaas-Holmes

HAVE MERCY
76.76

Still

3134

1. ___ Hide   me   now ___   un - der   your   wings. ___
(2. Find) rest,   my   soul, ___   in Christ a -   lone. ___

Cov - er   me ___   with - in   your   might - y   hand. ___
Know   his   power ___   in   qui - et - ness   and   trust. ___

Refrain

___ When the o-ceans rise and thun - ders roar, ___   I will soar with

You a - bove   the storm; ___   Fa-ther, you are king o - ver   the flood. ___

1

___   I will be still ___ and know you   are God. ___

2

2. Find   ___   and know you   are God. ___

WORDS: Reuben Morgan
MUSIC: Reuben Morgan

STILL
Irr. with Refrain

© 2002 Hillsong Publishing, admin. in the U.S. and Canada at EMICMGPublishing.com

3135   In God Alone

In God a-lone my soul can find rest and peace, in
God my peace and joy. On - ly in God my
soul can find its rest, find its rest and peace.

WORDS: Based on Psalm 62:1
MUSIC: Jacques Berthier

IN GOD ALONE
11 6.10 5

3136   In the Quiet of This Moment

In the qui - et _____ of this mo - ment _____ there is

joy. _____ In the qui - et _____ of this

WORDS: Dean McIntyre
MUSIC: Dean McIntyre

QUIET MOMENT
11 11.7 7 11

moment _____ there is hope. _____ In our doubt and in our fear, Ho-ly Spir-it now draw near; bring your com-fort and your cheer to long-ing hearts. _____

Lord Jesus Christ, Your Light Shines 3137
(*Jésus le Christ*)

Lord Je-sus Christ, your light shines with-in us. Let not my doubts nor my dark-ness speak to me. Lord Je-sus Christ, your light shines with-in us. Let my heart al-ways wel-come your love.

WORDS: Jacques Berthier
MUSIC: Jacques Berthier

JÉSUS LE CHRIST
10 11.10 9

3138

Confession

WORDS: j. Snodgrass
MUSIC: Isaac Everett

CONFESSION
Irr.

3139 We Cannot Measure How You Heal

1. We can - not meas - ure how you heal or
2. The pain that will not go a - way, the
3. So some have come who need your help and

an - swer ev - ery suf - ferer's prayer, yet
guilt that clings from things long past, the
some have come to make a - mends, as

we be - lieve your grace re - sponds where
fear of what the fu - ture holds are
hands which shaped and saved the world are

faith and doubt u - nite to care. Your hands, though
pres - ent as if meant to last. But pres - ent,
pres - ent in the touch of friends. Lord, let your

blood - ied on the cross, sur - vive to hold and
too, is love which tends the hurt we nev - er
Spir - it meet us here to mend the bod - y,

heal and warn, to car - ry all through death to
hope to find, the pri - vate ag - o - nies in -
mind and soul, to dis - en - tan - gle peace from

life and cra - dle chil - dren yet un - born.
side, the mem - o - ries that haunt the mind.
pain and make your bro - ken peo - ple whole.

WORDS: John L. Bell   CANDLER
MUSIC: Traditional Scottish melody   LMD

Words © 1989 WGRG, The Iona Community (Scotland), admin. by GIA Publications, Inc.

Give Me Jesus

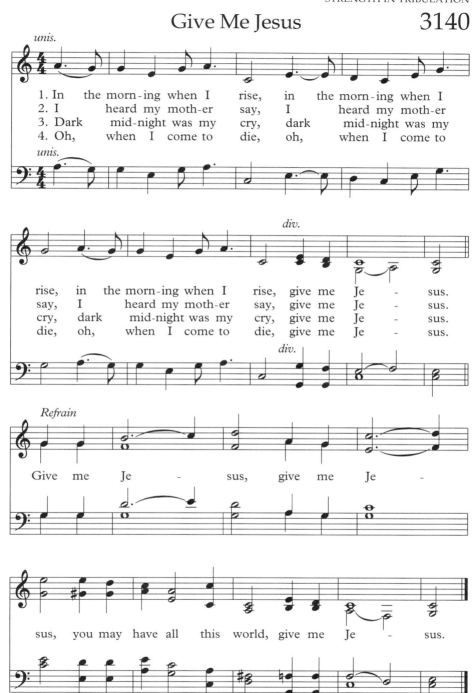

unis.

1. In the morn-ing when I rise, in the morn-ing when I
2. I heard my moth-er say, I heard my moth-er
3. Dark mid-night was my cry, dark mid-night was my
4. Oh, when I come to die, oh, when I come to

unis.

div.

rise, in the morn-ing when I rise, give me Je - sus.
say, I heard my moth-er say, give me Je - sus.
cry, dark mid-night was my cry, give me Je - sus.
die, oh, when I come to die, give me Je - sus.

div.

Refrain

Give me Je - sus, give me Je -

sus, you may have all this world, give me Je - sus.

WORDS: African American spiritual
MUSIC: African American spiritual, harm. by Verolga Nix

GIVE ME JESUS
66.64 with Refrain

Harm. © 1981 Abingdon Press, admin. by The Copyright Company

3141 Holy Darkness

Refrain

Ho - ly dark - ness, bless - ed night, heav-en's an - swer hid-den from our sight. As we a - wait you, O God of si - lence, we em - brace your ho - ly night.

Fine

Stanzas 1-3

1. I have tried you in fires of af - flic - tion, I have taught your soul to grieve. In the bar - ren soil of your lone - li - ness, there I will plant my seed.
2. I have taught you the price of com - pas - sion; you have stood be - fore the grave. Though my love can seem like a rag - ing storm, this is the love that saves.
3. Were you there when I raised up the moun - tains? Can you guide the morn-ing star? Does the hawk take flight when you give com - mand? Why do you doubt my power?

to Refrain

Stanzas 4-5

4. In your deep - est hour of dark - ness I will give you wealth un - told.
5. As the watch - man waits for morn - ing, and the bride a - waits her groom,

When the si - lence stills your so we wait to hear your

WORDS: Inspired by St. John of the Cross
MUSIC: Dan Schutte

HOLY DARKNESS
Irr. with Refrain

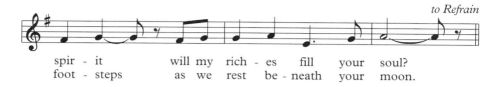

to Refrain

spir - it will my rich - es fill your soul?
foot - steps as we rest be - neath your moon.

I Love the Lord

3142

1. I love the Lord; he heard my cry and pit - ied
2. I love the Lord; he heard my cry and chased my

ev - ery groan. Long as I live and trou - bles
grief a - way. O let my heart no more des -

rise, I'll has - ten to his throne.
pair while I have breath to pray.

WORDS: Psalm 116:1-2; vers. Isaac Watts
MUSIC: African American spiritual; arr. by Richard Smallwood

I LOVE THE LORD
CM

3143 Jesus, You Are the New Day

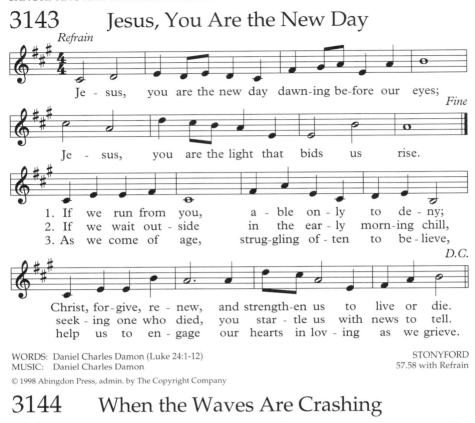

Refrain

Je - sus, you are the new day dawn-ing be-fore our eyes;

Fine

Je - sus, you are the light that bids us rise.

1. If we run from you, a - ble on - ly to de - ny;
2. If we wait out - side in the ear - ly morn-ing chill,
3. As we come of age, strug-gling of - ten to be - lieve,

D.C.

Christ, for - give, re - new, and strength-en us to live or die.
seek - ing one who died, you star - tle us with news to tell.
help us to en - gage our hearts in lov - ing as we grieve.

WORDS: Daniel Charles Damon (Luke 24:1-12)   STONYFORD
MUSIC: Daniel Charles Damon   57.58 with Refrain

© 1998 Abingdon Press, admin. by The Copyright Company

3144 When the Waves Are Crashing

1. When the waves are crash-ing and my faith is drown-ing, though I
2. When dark clouds have gath-ered and my love is bat-tered, though I

may for - get you, hold me, Lord. When the
may de - sert you, hold me, Lord. Faith may

cliffs are steep-est and my hope is weak-est, though I
be e - ter - nal, hope will last for - ev - er; great-er

fail to trust you, hold me, Lord. ___
still is love that holds me, Lord. ___

WORDS: Gareth Hill   BLUE MOOD
MUSIC: Jackson Henry   66.63 D

Words © 2007 Hope Publishing Company; music © 2011 Jackson Henry

Breath of God, Breath of Peace 3145

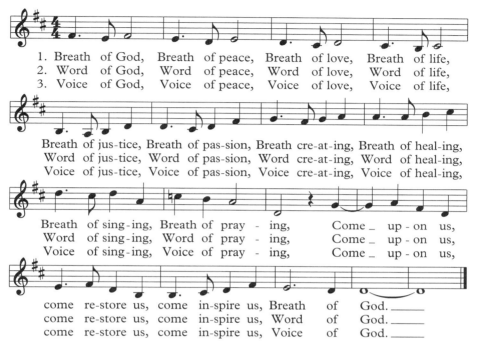

1. Breath of God, Breath of peace, Breath of love, Breath of life,
2. Word of God, Word of peace, Word of love, Word of life,
3. Voice of God, Voice of peace, Voice of love, Voice of life,

Breath of jus-tice, Breath of pas-sion, Breath cre-at-ing, Breath of heal-ing,
Word of jus-tice, Word of pas-sion, Word cre-at-ing, Word of heal-ing,
Voice of jus-tice, Voice of pas-sion, Voice cre-at-ing, Voice of heal-ing,

Breath of sing-ing, Breath of pray - ing, Come _ up - on us,
Word of sing-ing, Word of pray - ing, Come _ up - on us,
Voice of sing-ing, Voice of pray - ing, Come _ up - on us,

come re-store us, come in-spire us, Breath of God._____
come re-store us, come in-spire us, Word of God._____
come re-store us, come in-spire us, Voice of God._____

WORDS: Adam M. L. Tice
MUSIC: Sally Ann Morris

© 2009 GIA Publications, Inc.

PATTERNS
66.88.887

O Breath of Life 3146

1. O Breath of life, come sweep - ing through us, re - vive your
2. O Wind of God, come bend us, break us, till hum - bly
3. O Breath of love, come breathe with - in us, re - new - ing

church with life and power. O Breath of life, come cleanse, re -
we con-fess our need. Then in your ten - der - ness re -
thought and will and heart. Come, love of Christ, a - fresh to

new us, and fit your church to meet this hour.
make us; re-vive, re - store, for this we plead.
win us; re-vive your church in ev - ery part.

WORDS: Bessie Porter Head
MUSIC: Carlton R. Young

Music © 2008 Abingdon Press, admin. by The Copyright Company

ADIEU
98.98

3147 Built on a Rock

1. Built on a rock the Church shall stand,
2. Sure - ly in tem - ples made with hands
3. We are God's house of liv - ing stones,
4. Still we our earth - ly tem - ples raise
5. Here stands the font be - fore our eyes
6. Grant then, O God, where - e'er we go,

e - ven when stee - ples are fall - ing;
Al - might - y God is now dwell - ing;
built for God's own ha - bi - ta - tion;
hous - es where God can draw near us;
tell - ing how God has re - ceived us;
that, when the church bells are ring - ing,

crum - bled have spires in ev - ery land, bells still are
high a - bove earth his tem - ple stands, all earth - ly
he, through bap - tis - mal grace, us owns, heirs of a
plac - es for wor - ship, prayer, and praise, beau - ty and
th'al - tar re - calls Christ's sac - ri - fice and what his
man - y in faith may come to know this mes - sage

WORDS: Nikolai F. S. Grundtvig; trans. by Carl Doving;
adapt. by Dean McIntyre
MUSIC: Ludwig M. Lindeman

KIRKEN DEN ER ET GAMMELT HUS
88.88.88.8

Adapt. © 2004 The General Board of Discipleship of The United Methodist Church

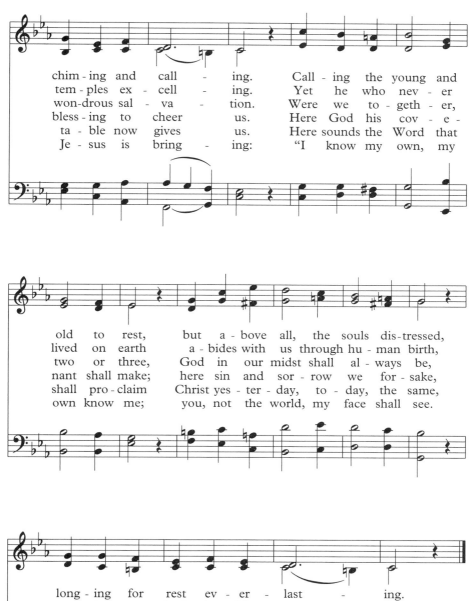

3148 There's a Spirit of Love in This Place

1. There's a spir - it of love in this place, there's a
(2. There's the) pres - ence of peace in this room, there's the

spir - it of love in this place. You can't
pres - ence of peace in this room. In God's

see it, but it's there just as pre-cious as the air. There's a
ten-der-ness is found peace that pass - es hu-man bounds. There's the

spir - it of love in this place. O al - le -
pres - ence of peace in this room.

lu - ia, sing al - le - lu - ia! We bless your ho - ly

name. O al - le - lu - ia, sing al - le - lu - ia! There's a

1.
spir - it of love in this place.

2.
2. There's the place.

WORDS: Mark A. Miller
MUSIC: Mark A. Miller

MEDEMA
Irr.

A Place at the Table

3149

1. For ev-ery-one born, a place at the ta - ble, for
2. For wom-an and man, a place at the ta - ble, re -
3. For young and for old, a place at the ta - ble, a
4. For just and un - just, a place at the ta - ble, a -
5. For ev-ery-one born, a place at the ta - ble, to

ev-ery-one born, clean wa-ter and bread, __ a shel-ter, a
vis-ing the roles, de-cid-ing the share, __ with wis-dom and
voice to be heard, a part in the song, __ the hands of a
bus-er, a - bused, with need to for-give, __ in an-ger, in
live with-out fear, and sim-ply to be, ____ to work, to speak

space, a safe place for grow - ing, for ev - ery-one born, a
grace, di - vid - ing the pow - er, for wom - an and man, a
child in hands that are wrin - kled, for young and for old, the
hurt, a mind-set of mer - cy, for just and un - just, a
out, to wit - ness and wor - ship, for ev - ery-one born, the

Refrain

star o - ver - head. ____
sys - tem that's fair. ____
right to be - long. ____ And God will de - light ____ when
new way to live. ____
right to be free. ____

we are cre-a - tors of jus-tice and joy, ____ yes, God will de-

light ____ when we are cre-a - tors of jus - tice, ____

jus - tice and joy! ____

WORDS: Shirley Erena Murray
MUSIC: Lori True

PLACE AT THE TABLE
11 10.11 10 with Refrain

Words © 1998 Hope Publishing Company; music © 2001 GIA Publications, Inc.

3150 Father, We Have Heard You Calling

1. Fa - ther, we have heard you call - ing to your
2. Je - sus Christ, our faith's per - fec - ter, priest and
3. Ho - ly Spir - it, fire of heav - en, fall up -
4. Praise we bring to God the Fa - ther, praise we

church in ev - ery age; for a sign of true de -
ad - vo - cate a - bove. We would reach our bro - ken
on us here to - day. Bring re - lease, bring tears, bring
bring to God the Son, praise to God the Ho - ly

vo - tion for a sac - ri - fice of praise.
na - tion with the truth of your great love.
pas - sion, then trans - form your church, we pray.
Spir - it, praise to you, the three in one.

In this place where you have brought us, may we
So trans - form our fee - ble wit - ness, may we
As you pour your grace up - on us, may we
Tri - ni - ty of love in - spire us, may we

WORDS: Gareth Hill
MUSIC: Rowland H. Prichard; harm. from *The English Hymnal*
Words © 2005 Hope Publishing Company

HYFRYDOL
87.87 D

al - ways seek to be one in love and one in
al - ways live to be one in love and one in
al - ways thirst to be one in love and one in
al - ways strive to be one in love and one in

wor - ship — chil - dren of e - ter - ni - ty.
wor - ship — chil - dren of e - ter - ni - ty.
wor - ship — chil - dren of e - ter - ni - ty.
wor - ship — chil - dren of e - ter - ni - ty.

The Jesus in Me   3151

The Je - sus in me loves the Je - sus in you, the
El Je - sus en mi al - ma el Je - sus en ti, El

Je - sus in me loves the Je - sus in you, so eas - y,
Je - sus en mi al - ma el Je - sus en ti tan fa - cil,

so eas - y, so eas-
tan fa - cil, tan fa -

y, so eas-y to love.
cil, tan fa-cil a - mor.

WORDS: Anonymous
MUSIC: Anonymous

SO EASY
Irr.

3152 Welcome

1. Let's walk to-geth - er for a while and ask where we be - gin___ to build a world where love can grow and hope can en - ter in, ___ ___ to be the hands of heal - ing and to plant the seed of peace, _

2. Let's talk to-geth - er of a time when we will share a feast, _ where pride and pow - er kneel to serve the lone - ly and the least, _ ___ and joy will set the ta - ble as we join our hands to pray, ___

3. Let's dream to-geth - er of the day when earth and heaven are one, _ a ci - ty built of love and light, the new Je - ru - sa - lem, _ where our mourn - ing turns to danc - ing, ev - ery crea - ture lifts its voice, _

Refrain

sing-ing wel - come, sing-ing wel - come, cry-ing wel - come, wel-come to this place. You're in - vit - ed to come and know God's grace. All are wel - come the

WORDS: Laurie Zelman
MUSIC: Mark A. Miller

WELCOME
Irr. with Refrain

love of God to share _____ 'cause all of us are wel-come here; _

___ all are wel-come in this place. _____

O God, in Whom We Live 3153

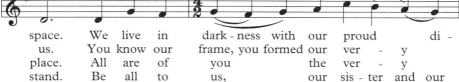

1. O God, in whom we live and move and have our
2. We seek your face, your ways, in far - off
3. No work of ours, these fee - ble, fad - ing
4. Work now this day our blind - ed eyes to
5. Be, liv - ing God not made by hands of

be - ing, you set the bounds of time and
pla - ces, though you are near to each of
ob - jects, can fill our hearts, nor take your
o - pen, make our hearts quick to un - der -
hu - mans, no more to us a God un -

space. We live in dark - ness with our proud di -
us. You know our frame, you formed our ver - y
place. All are of you the ver - y
stand. Be all to us, our sis - ter and our
known; that we to - geth - er drink joy un -

vi - sions, yet are in you one blood, one race.
fa - ces, you call us each to see your light.
off - spring, in ev - ery - one we see your face.
broth - er, touch us in one an - oth - er's hand.
end - ing, as we sing prais - es 'round your throne!

WORDS: William P. Gorton
MUSIC: William P. Gorton
© 2007 William P. Gorton

AREOPAGUS
Irr.

3154   Draw the Circle Wide

Draw the cir - cle, draw the cir - cle wide. Draw the

cir-cle, draw the cir-cle wide. No one stands a-lone, we'll stand side by

side. Draw the cir-cle, draw the cir - cle wide. Draw the

wide. Draw the cir-cle wide, draw it wid-er still. Let this

be our song: no one stands a-lone. Stand-ing side by side,

draw the cir-cle, draw the cir - cle wide. Draw the

WORDS: Gordon Light
MUSIC: Mark A. Miller

DRAW THE CIRCLE
Irr.

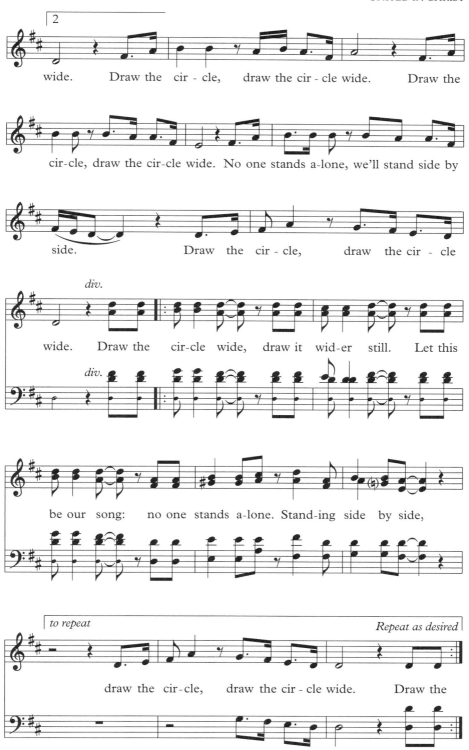

Draw the cir-cle, draw the cir-cle wide. Draw the

molto rit.

cir - cle, draw the cir - cle wide.

3155 The Lord of Life, a Vine Is He

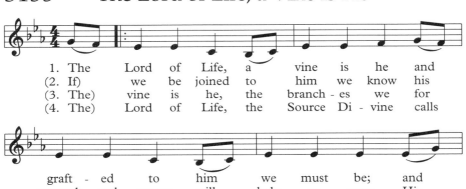

1. The Lord of Life, a vine is he and
(2. If) we be joined to him we know his
(3. The) vine is he, the branch - es we for
(4. The) Lord of Life, the Source Di - vine calls

graft - ed to him we must be; and
strength and power will help us grow. His
now and to e - ter - ni - ty. His
us to come, with him en - twine. Will

thus we yield a - bun-dant-ly sweet fruit for all to
Spir - it's grace through us will flow to prune and shape us
word sown deep in us will be both sun and rain... suf -
we, un - hear - ing, dare de-cline the call of Christ, the

taste and see.   2. If
as   we   go.   3. The
fi - cien - cy.   4. The

One True Vine?

WORDS: Mary Kay Beall
MUSIC: John Carter
© 2005 Hope Publishing Company

LATHAM
LM

One Is the Body

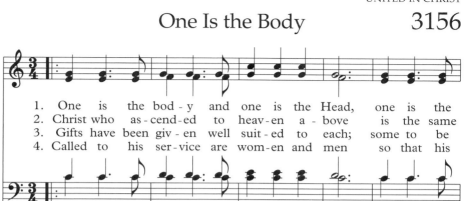

1. One is the bod-y and one is the Head, one is the
2. Christ who as-cend-ed to heav-en a - bove is the same
3. Gifts have been giv-en well suit-ed to each; some to be
4. Called to his ser-vice are wom-en and men so that his

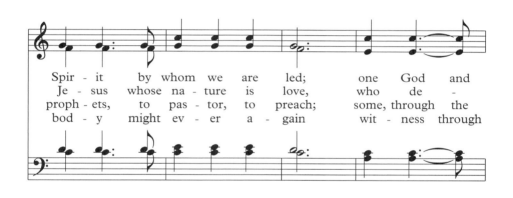

Spir - it by whom we are led; one God and
Je - sus whose na - ture is love, who de -
proph - ets, to pas - tor, to preach; some, through the
bod - y might ev - er a - gain wit - ness through

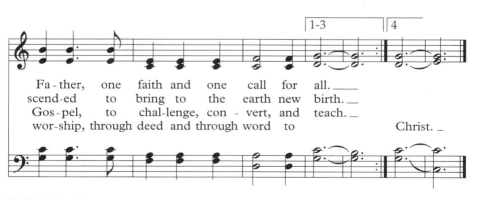

1-3 · 4

Fa - ther, one faith and one call for all. ____
scend-ed to bring to the earth new birth. __
Gos - pel, to chal-lenge, con - vert, and teach. __
wor-ship, through deed and through word to Christ. _

WORDS: John Bell
MUSIC: John Bell

ONE IS THE BODY
Irr.

3157 Come, Let Us Dream

1. Come, let us dream God's dream a -
2. The lame shall walk, the blind shall
3. When ha - tred ends and war shall
4. But know the cost of claim - ing
5. Proph - ets are scorned in their own

gain. Come, one and all, let us as -
see, the doors swing wide, all pri - soners
cease, so all may dwell in deep - est
sight of God's new day, of wrongs made
lands and mar - tyrs slain by right - eous

cend the moun - tain - top where those of
free, the low - ly raised, the proud brought
peace, then be as - sured the time is
right, for some have paid the high - est
hands; though dream - ers die, the dream will

old saw God's new day on earth un - fold.
low. This is God's dream: let jus - tice flow.
near when per - fect love casts out all fear.
price, their lives for us, a sac - ri - fice.
live, for we have yet our lives to give.

WORDS: John Middleton
MUSIC: English folk melody
O WALY WALY
LM

Words © 2004 John Middleton

3158 Go to the World

1. Go to the world! Go in - to all the earth. Go
2. Go to the world! Go in - to ev - ery place.
3. Go to the world! Go strug - gle, bless and pray; the
4. Go to the world! Go as the ones I send, for

WORDS: Sylvia G. Dunstan
MUSIC: Ralph Vaughan Williams
SINE NOMINE
10 10 10 with Alleluias

Words © 1991 GIA Publications, Inc.

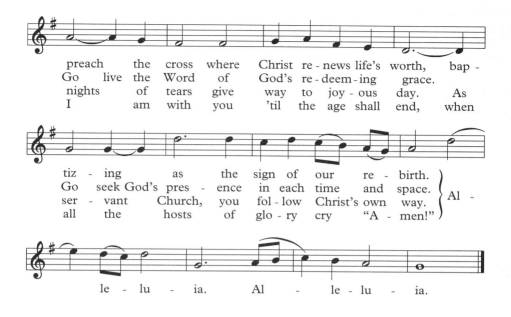

preach the cross where Christ re-news life's worth, bap-
Go live the Word of God's re-deem-ing grace.
nights of tears give way to joy-ous day. As
I am with you 'til the age shall end, when

tiz - ing as the sign of our re - birth.
Go seek God's pres - ence in each time and space. } Al -
ser - vant Church, you fol - low Christ's own way.
all the hosts of glo - ry cry "A - men!"

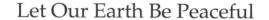

le - lu - ia. Al - le - lu - ia.

Let Our Earth Be Peaceful 3159

1. Let our earth be peace - ful, let our hearts be
2. Let our ways be mind - ful, mend-ing what is
3. Let our lives be fruit - ful, beau - ti - ful and

[1, 2]

hope - ful, let our hands be gen - tle for the love of
hurt - ful, do-ing what is need - ful for the love of
play - ful, ev - ery day be thank - ful

[3]

God.
God.

for the love of God.

WORDS: Shirley Erena Murray
MUSIC: Carlton R. Young

RAYMOND
66.65

3160

We Will Follow
(Somlandela)

We will fol-low, we will fol-low Je - sus. We will fol - low,
Som - lan - de - la, som-lan-del' u - Je - su. Som - lan - de - la,

we will fol-low him. We will fol - low, we will fol-low Je - sus.
yon - ke in - da - wo. Som - lan - de - la, som-lan-del' u - Je - su.

To Repeat
Leader: We will fol-low.
Som-lan-de - la.

Song Ending

Wher-ev-er he leads us we will fol - low.
La - pho e - ya - kho - na som-lan - de - la.

fol - low.
de - la.

WORDS: Traditional Zulu
MUSIC: Traditional Zulu; arr. by Dean McIntyre

SOMLANDELA
10 9.10 10

Arr. © 2005 The General Board of Discipleship of The United Methodist Church

3161 Gracious Creator of Sea and of Land

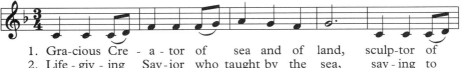

1. Gra - cious Cre - a - tor of sea and of land, sculp-tor of
2. Life - giv - ing Sav - ior who taught by the sea, say - ing to
3. Spir - it of Pen - te - cost, still blow-ing free, show us your

WORDS: John Thornburg
MUSIC: Daniel Charles Damon

MONA WEST
10 10.10 10

© 2008 Abingdon Press, admin. by The Copyright Company

cor - al and mill - er of sand, stretch out your hand, part the
fish - er - folk, "Come, fol - low me," send us to gath - er the
vi - sion of all we can be. Call us to bold - ness, to

seas of our lives. Lead us to free - dom and o - pen our eyes.
out - casts, the least. Make us your aides at the great jus - tice feast.
good - ness, to prayer. Sum - mon our cour - age, our dream - ing, our care.

Stand in Awe

3162

Stand in awe of the one who hears the cry of the poor. _

Stand in awe of the one who will pro - vide. _____

Stand in awe of the one who hears the cry of the poor, _

_ for they shall eat and be sat - is - fied. _____

WORDS: Psalm 22:22-30, adapt. by Bret Hesla
MUSIC: Bret Hesla

STAND IN AWE
13 10.13 9

3163 Walking in the Light of God

Refrain

Walk in the light, walk in the light,

To Stanzas
Last time - Fine

walk in the light, walk-ing in the light of God.

1. Walk, walk, walk, walk, walk-ing in the light of God.

To Refrain

Walk, walk, walk, walk, walk-ing in the light of God.

WORDS: Traditional Zulu
MUSIC: Traditional Zulu; arr. by Dean McIntyre

HAMBA
Irr. with Refrain

2. 'Ham-ba, 'ham-ba, 'ham-ba, 'ham-ba, walk-ing in the light of God.

To Refrain

'Ham-ba, 'ham-ba, 'ham-ba, 'ham-ba, walk-ing in the light of God.

3. 'Ham - ba koo kah nigh nee, 'ham - ba koo kah nigh nee,

To Refrain

'ham - ba koo kah nigh nee, walk-ing in the light of God.

3164 Down to the River to Pray

1. As I went down to the riv-er to pray,
stud-y-in' a-bout that good ole way and who shall wear the
{ star - ry crown, }
{ robe and crown, } good Lord, show me the way.

O *sis - ters, let's go down, let's go down, come on down.

* 2. brothers
  3. fathers
  4. mothers
  5. sinners

WORDS: Southern USA folk song
MUSIC: Southern USA folk song; transcribed by Jackson Henry

DOWN TO THE RIVER
Irr.

Transcription © 2011 Jackson Henry

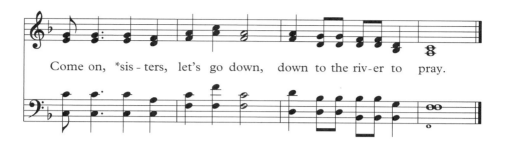

Come on, *sis - ters, let's go down, down to the riv-er to pray.

Take Me to the Water 3165

1. Take me to the wa - ter. Take me to the wa -
2. None but the right - eous, none but the right -
3. I love Je - sus, I love Je -
4. He's my Sav - ior. He's my Sav -

ter. Take me to the wa - ter to be bap - tized.
eous, none but the right - eous shall see God.
sus, I love Je - sus, yes, I do.
ior. He's my Sav - ior, yes, he is.

WORDS: African American spiritual
MUSIC: African American spiritual

TAKE ME TO THE WATER
Irr.

3166 Author of Life Divine

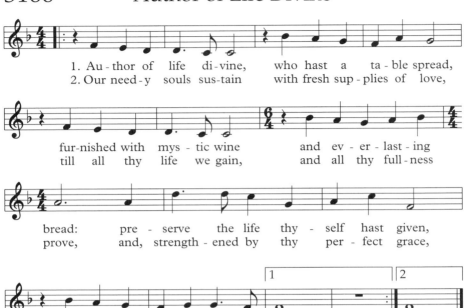

1. Au-thor of life di-vine, who hast a ta-ble spread,
2. Our need-y souls sus-tain with fresh sup-plies of love,

fur-nished with mys-tic wine and ev-er-last-ing
till all thy life we gain, and all thy full-ness

bread: pre-serve the life thy-self hast given,
prove, and, strength-ened by thy per-fect grace,

1
and feed and train us up for heaven.
be-hold with-out a veil thy

2
face.

WORDS: Charles Wesley
MUSIC: Jackson Henry
Music © 2011 Jackson Henry

AUTHOR
66.66.88

3167 Feed Us, Lord

1. Feed us, Lord. Feed us, Lord. In the bro-ken bread,
2. Quench us, Lord. Quench us, Lord. On this thirst-y ground,
3. Fill us, Lord. Fill us, Lord, with the bread and wine
4. Lead us, Lord. Lead us, Lord. Nour-ished here by Christ;

be re-vealed a-gain. Come and feed our hearts, O Lord.
may your love flow down. Come and quench our hearts, O Lord.
of the ris-en Christ. Come and fill our hearts, O Lord.
giv-en strength for life. Come and lead our hearts, O Lord.

WORDS: Greg Scheer
MUSIC: Greg Scheer
© 2007 Greg Scheer

FEED US
33.55.7

Come to the Table of Grace 3168

Come to the ta-ble of grace.____ Come to the
ta-ble of grace.____ This is God's ta-ble; it's not yours or
mine. Come to the ta-ble of grace._____

2. Come to the table of peace...
3. Come to the table of love...
4. Come to the table of joy...

WORDS: Barbara Hamm
MUSIC: Barbara Hamm
© 2008 Barbara Hamm

TABLE OF GRACE
7 7.10 7

You Feed Us, Gentle Savior 3169

1. You feed us, gen-tle Sav-ior, the bread that makes us whole,
2. You bind us, gen-tle Sav-ior, and weave us in-to one,
3. You call us, gen-tle Sav-ior, and send us in your name.

the wine of your com-pas-sion poured out in-to our soul.
one flesh and blood made ho-ly, the Bod-y of your Son.
You teach and heal and show us how we can do the same.

The food of your own pres-ence, your Spir-it, strong, with-in,
We gath-er here in hun-ger, one hun-ger, all the same;
So, strength-ened by your Spir-it and nour-ished by your grace,

the grace that heals us deep-ly and o-ver-comes our sin.
and with one grace you bless us to-geth-er in his name.
we go to be your pres-ence in love, in ev-ery place.

WORDS: Steve Garnaas-Holmes
MUSIC: Hal H. Hopson
Words © 2009 Steve Garnaas-Holmes; music © 1983 Hope Publishing Company

MERLE'S TUNE
76.76 D

3170   What Feast of Love

1. What feast of love is of-fered here, what ban-quet come from heav-en?
2. What light of truth is of-fered here, what cov - e - nant from heav-en?
3. What wine of love is of-fered here, what crim-son drink from heav-en?

What food of ev - er - last-ing life, what gra - cious gift is giv - en?
What hope of ev - er - last-ing life, what won-drous word is giv - en?
What stream of ev - er - last-ing life, what pre - cious blood is giv - en?

This, this is Christ the king, the bread come down from heav - en.
This, this is Christ the king, the sun come down from heav - en.
This, this is Christ the king, the sweet - est wine of heav - en.

Oh, taste and see and sing! How sweet the man - na giv - en!
Oh, see and hear and sing! The Word of God is giv - en!
Oh, taste and see and sing! The Son of God is giv - en!

WORDS: Delores Dufner
MUSIC: English melody, 16th cent.

GREENSLEEVES
87.87.67.67

Communion Setting
(Sanctus and Benedictus)

3171-a

Ho - ly, ho - ly, ho - ly Lord, God of power and might,

heav - en and earth are full of your glo - ry. Ho -

san - na in the high - est. Bless-ed is he who comes in the

name of the Lord. Ho - san - na in the high - est.

WORDS: From *The United Methodist Hymnal*
MUSIC: Sally Ahner
Music © 1983 Sally Ahner

SANCTUS (AHNER)
Irr.

(Memorial Acclamation)

3171-b

Christ has died, Christ is ris - en, Christ will come a - gain.

WORDS: From *The United Methodist Hymnal*
MUSIC: Sally Ahner
Music © 1983 Sally Ahner

ACCLAMATION (AHNER)
Irr.

(Amen)

3171-c

A - men, A - men, A - men.

WORDS: From *The United Methodist Hymnal*
MUSIC: Sally Ahner
Music © 1988, 1996 Sally Ahner

AMEN (AHNER)
Irr.

3172-a Communion Setting
(Holy, Holy, Holy)

Leader *All*

Ho - ly, ho - ly, ho - ly Lord, ho - ly, ho - ly, ho - ly Lord,

Leader *All*

God of pow - er and might, God of pow - er and might.

Leader

Heav - en and earth are full of your glo - ry.

All *Leader*

Heav - en and earth are full of your glo - ry. Ho -

All

san - na in the high - est. Ho -

san - na in the high - est.

Leader *All*

Bless-ed is the one who comes, bless-ed is the one who comes,

Leader *All* *Leader*

in the name of the Lord, in the name of the Lord. Ho -

WORDS: From *The United Methodist Hymnal* SANCTUS (HENRY)
MUSIC: Jackson Henry Irr.

Music © 2011 Jackson Henry

san - na, ho-san - na, ho - san - na in the high - est.

(Christ Has Died) 3172-b

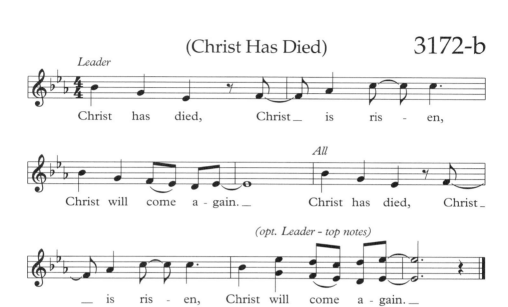

Leader

Christ has died, Christ ___ is ris - en,

All

Christ will come a - gain. ___ Christ has died, Christ ___

(opt. Leader - top notes)

___ is ris - en, Christ will come a - gain. ___

WORDS: From *The United Methodist Hymnal*
MUSIC: Jackson Henry
Music © 2011 Jackson Henry

ACCLAMATION (HENRY)
Irr.

(Amen) 3172-c

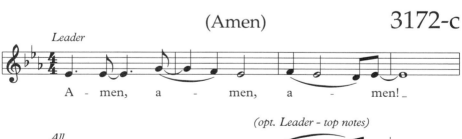

Leader

A - men, a - men, a - men! ___

(opt. Leader - top notes)

All

A - men, a - men, a - men! ___

WORDS: From *The United Methodist Hymnal*
MUSIC: Jackson Henry
Music © 2011 Jackson Henry

AMEN (HENRY)
Irr.

3173

Table of Plenty

Refrain

Come to the feast of heav-en and earth! Come to the ta-

ble of plen - ty! God will pro-vide for

all that we need here at the ta - ble of plen -

1-4 *to Stanzas* ‖ *5* *Fine*

ty. ty.

1. O come and sit at my ta - ble where
2. O come and eat with-out mon - ey;
3. My bread will ev - er sus - tain you through
4. Your fields will flow - er in full - ness; your

saints and sin - ners are friends. I wait to
come to drink with-out price. My feast of
days of sor - row and woe. My wine will
homes will flour - ish in peace. For I, the

wel - come the lost and lone - ly to share the
glad - ness will feed your spir - it with faith and
flow like a sea of glad - ness to flood the
giv - er of home and har - vest, will send my

WORDS: Dan Schutte
MUSIC: Dan Schutte
© 1992 Daniel L. Schutte, admin. by OCP

PLENTY
Irr. with Refrain

D.C.

cup of my love. _____
full - ness of life. _____
depths of your soul. _____
rain on the soil. _____

Christ, We Are Blest

3174

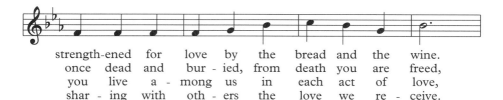

1. Christ, we are blest as we gath - er to dine,
2. You laid your life down like sow - ing a seed;
3. Christ, you are ris - en, but not far a - bove:
4. Je - sus, you feed us, then bid us to leave,

strength-ened for love by the bread and the wine.
once dead and bur - ied, from death you are freed,
you live a - mong us in each act of love,
shar - ing with oth - ers the love we re - ceive.

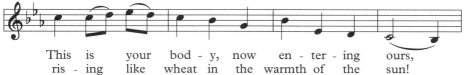

This is your bod - y, now en - ter - ing ours,
ris - ing like wheat in the warmth of the sun!
in ev - ery deed of com - pas - sion you rise,
We are your bod - y, sent by your com - mand,

strong with your lov - ing, mi - rac - u - lous powers.
Christ, you are ris - en! New life has be - gun!
liv - ing in flesh we can see with our eyes.
mak - ing love real as the bread in our hands.

WORDS: Steve Garnaas-Holmes
MUSIC: Irish folk melody
Words © 2009 Steve Garnaas-Holmes

SLANE
10 10.10 10

3175 Christ, We Come with Joy and Gladness

1. Christ, we come with joy and glad-ness as we wit-ness love made new;
2. Hope and joy and love a-bound-ing, this our prayer for their suc-cess;

hear the prayers of two u-nit-ed as their lives are
let the lives of these, our loved ones, know the joy of

joined in you. Seek-ing you to bond their mar-riage,
those you bless. Christ, our Shep-herd, tend and keep them,

they are trust-ing you to be in ____ the cord that
and your peace and care be known. May ____ the world in

can't be bro-ken, giv-ing them the strength of three.
which you place them praise you as their love is shown.

WORDS: Constance M. Cherry
MUSIC: Ludwig van Beethoven; arr. by Edward Hodges
Words © 1999 Hope Publishing Company

HYMN TO JOY
87.87D

Come, Now Is the Time to Worship 3176

Come, now is the time to wor - ship. _

Come, now is the time to give _ your heart. _

Come, just as you are to wor - ship. _

Last time to Coda

Come, just as you are be - fore _ your God, _

come. One day ev - ery tongue will con - fess _

_ you are God. One day ev - ery knee will bow. _

Still the great - est treas - ure re - mains _ for those who glad-

1. ly choose you now. _
2. _
D.S. 3. _

CODA

Come. Come. Come.

WORDS: Brian Doerksen
MUSIC: Brian Doerksen

NOW IS THE TIME
Irr.

3177 Here I Am to Worship

1. Light of the world, you stepped down in-to dark-ness,
2. King of all days, O so high-ly ex-alt-ed,

o-pened my eyes, let me see. Beau-ty that made this
glo-rious in heav-en a-bove. Hum-bly you came to the

heart a-dore you, hope of a life spent with you.
earth you cre-at-ed, all for love's sake be-came poor.

Here I am to wor-ship, here I am to bow down, here I am to

say that you're my God.__ You're al-to-geth-er love-ly, al-to-geth-er

Third time to Coda

wor-thy, al-to-geth-er won-der-ful to me.__

And I'll nev-er know how much__ it cost to see__

__ my sin up-on__ that cross. I'll nev-er know how much__

__ it cost to see__ my sin up-on__ that cross. I'll nev-

WORDS: Tim Hughes
MUSIC: Tim Hughes

HERE I AM TO WORSHIP
Irr.

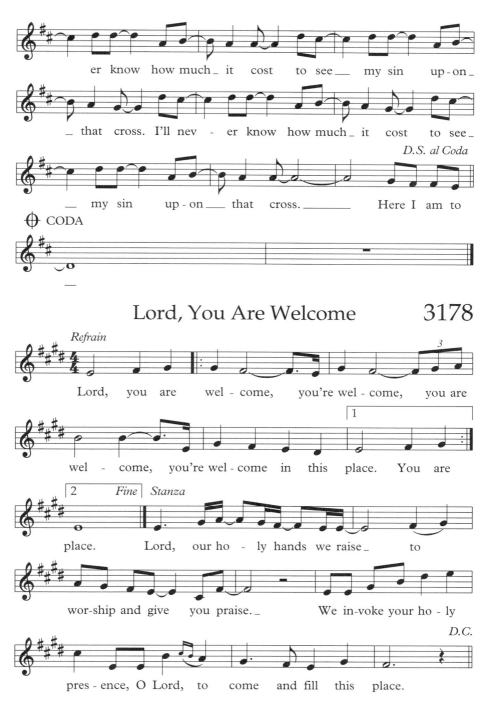

er know how much_ it cost to see_ my sin up-on_

_ that cross. I'll nev - er know how much_ it cost to see_

D.S. al Coda

_ my sin up-on_ that cross._____ Here I am to

CODA

Lord, You Are Welcome 3178

Refrain

Lord, you are wel - come, you're wel - come, you are

wel - come, you're wel - come in this place. You are

Fine *Stanza*

place. Lord, our ho - ly hands we raise_ to

wor-ship and give you praise._ We in-voke your ho - ly

D.C.

pres - ence, O Lord, to come and fill this place.

WORDS: Warren Jones
MUSIC: Warren Jones; arr. by Nolan Williams, Jr.
Words © Warren Jones; arr. © 2000 GIA Publications, Inc.

YOU ARE WELCOME
Irr.

3179 The Risen Christ

1. O breath of God, come fill this place; re - vive our
2. O Word of God, so clear and true, re - new our
3. O love of God, so un - re - strained, re - fresh our
4. May God the Fa - ther, God the Son, and God the

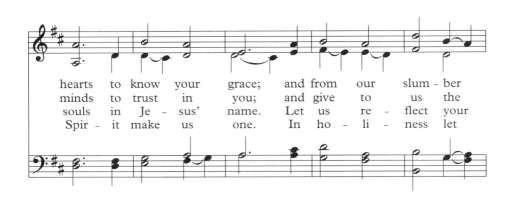

hearts to know your grace; and from our slum - ber
minds to trust in you; and give to us the
souls in Je - sus' name. Let us re - flect your
Spir - it make us one. In ho - li - ness let

make us rise that we may know the ris - en Christ.
bread of life that we may know the ris - en Christ.
sac - ri - fice that we may know the ris - en Christ.
us u - nite that we may know the ris - en Christ.

WORDS: Keith Getty and Phil Madeira   THE RISEN CHRIST
MUSIC: Keith Getty and Phil Madeira; arr. by Bruce Greer   LM

As We Part for the Towns and Cities 3180

As we part for the towns and ci - ties, where you
sum - mon us to go, guide us, Lord, give us strength and
cour - age, teach us all we need to know. Keep us
hum - ble, fixed on you, for-ev-er seek-ing, born a - new. Kin-dle
ho - ly fires with-in us; may your Ho - ly Spir - it glow.

WORDS: John Thornburg
MUSIC: Jackson Henry

CONNECTION
Irr.

Words © 2007 John Thornburg; music © 2011 Jackson Henry

Peace, Salaam, Shalom 3181

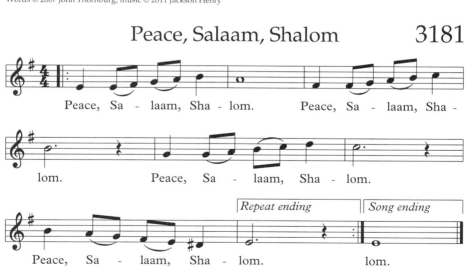

Peace, Sa - laam, Sha - lom. Peace, Sa - laam, Sha -
lom. Peace, Sa - laam, Sha - lom.

Repeat ending ||*Song ending*

Peace, Sa - laam, Sha - lom. lom.

WORDS: Traditional
MUSIC: Dean McIntyre

BEERSHEBA
55.55

Music © 2004 The General Board of Discipleship of The United Methodist Church

3182

Benediction Hymn

O Lord, now let your ser-vants de-part in peace, ac-cord-ing
to your gra-cious word. Our eyes have seen the glo-ry of sal-
va-tion pre-pared for all the peo-ple of the world. Now may the
Lord bless you and keep you and make his face to shine up-on

WORDS: Luke 2:28-32; Numbers 6:24-26
MUSIC: Traditional Irish melody; transcription by Dean McIntyre

LONDONDERRY AIR
Irr.

you; and may God lift his coun - te - nance up -

on you and give you bless-ed peace for now and ev - er - more.

As We Go — 3183

As we go, __ may your Spir-it go be - fore us. As we go, __

__ may we fol - low where you lead. May we

live what we have learned, share the mes-sage we have heard, and be a

light un - to the world as we go. __

WORDS: Jeremy Johnson
MUSIC: Jeremy Johnson

AS WE GO
Irr.

3184   Word of God, Speak

1. I'm find-ing my-self ___ at a loss for words, ___ and the
(2. I'm find-ing my-self) ___ in the midst of you, be-yond the

fun-ny thing is ___ it's o - kay. The last thing I need ___
mu - sic, be-yond the noise. ___ All that I need ___

___ is to be heard, ___ but to hear ___ what you would
___ is to be with You, and in the qui - et, I hear your

say. Word of God, speak. ___ Would you pour down like rain, ___
voice.

___ wash-ing my eyes ___ to see your maj-

es-ty, to be still and know ___ that you're in this place? ___

Third time to Coda

___ Please let me stay ___ and rest in your ho-

li - ness. Word of God, speak. ___

WORDS: Pete Kipley and Bart Millard
MUSIC: Pete Kipley and Bart Millard

WORD OF GOD, SPEAK
Irr.

D.S. al Coda

2. I'm find-ing my-self _ li-ness. Word of God, speak. _

CODA

li-ness. Word of God, speak. _

Word of God, speak. _

Send Us Your Spirit 3185

1. Send us your Spir - it, O Lord._____
2. Hold us with mer - cy, O Lord._____
3. Teach us your wis - dom, O Lord._____
4. Send us good sum - mer, O Lord._____

Eve - ning en - folds us and holds us too near.
Sor - row has spo - ken, has bro - ken our hearts.
Shad-ows have cloud-ed, have crowd-ed our sight.
Win - ters have chilled us and stilled us too long.

Wake the morn-ing light. Make our liv-ing bright.
Clothe us in your care. Be the life we bear.
Give us hearts that see. Set our lov-ing free.
Give us love's own fire. Be our true de - sire.

Shine on our dark-ness, O Lord.
Feed us and fill us, O Lord.
Hear us and help us, O Lord.
Send us your Spir - it, O Lord.

WORDS: Dan Schutte
MUSIC: Dan Schutte
© 1985 OCP

EVENING PRAYER
7 10.10 7

3186 Days of Elijah

1. These are the days of E-li-jah, de-
2. These are the days of E-ze-kiel, the

clar-ing the Word of the Lord. And
dry bones be-com-ing as flesh. And

these are the days of your ser-vant, Mo-ses;
these are the days of your ser-vant, Da-vid, re-

right-eous-ness be-ing re-stored. And
build-ing the tem-ple of praise. And

though these are days of great tri-als, of
these are the days of the har-vest; the

fam-ine and dark-ness and sword, still
fields are as white in the world. And

we are the voice in the des-ert cry-ing, "Pre-
we are your la-bor-ers in your vine-yard de-

Refrain

pare ye the way of the Lord." Be-hold he
clar-ing the Word of the Lord. Be-hold he

WORDS: Robin Mark
MUSIC: Robin Mark

DAYS OF ELIJAH
Irr.

comes rid-ing on the clouds,_ shin-ing like the sun_ _ at the trum-pet call. So lift your voice, it's the year of Ju-bi-lee. _ And out of Zi-on's hill sal - va - tion comes.

We Fall Down 3187

We fall down, we lay our crowns at the feet_ of Je-sus; the great-ness of mer-cy and love at the feet_ _ of Je - sus. And we cry, "Ho - ly, ho - ly, ho-ly." And we cry, "Ho - ly, ho - ly, ho - ly." And we cry, "Ho - ly, ho - ly, ho - ly is the Lamb."_

WORDS: Chris Tomlin
MUSIC: Chris Tomlin

WE FALL DOWN
Irr.

© 1998 worshiptogether.com Songs (ASCAP), admin. at EMICMGPublishing.com

3188

Hosanna

1. I see the King of glo - ry
2. I see a ge - ne - ra - tion

com-ing on the clouds with fire. __ The whole earth shakes, __
ris-ing up to take their place __ with self - less faith, __

__ the whole earth shakes. __ I see his love and mer-
__ with self - less faith. __ I see a near re - vi-

cy wash - ing o - ver all our sin. __
val stir - ring as we pray and seek. __

Refrain

__ The peo - ple sing, __ the peo - ple sing. __ Ho-san-
__ We're on our knees, __ we're on our knees. __

na ho-san - na. Ho-san-na in the high-est.

Third time to Coda ⊕

Ho-san - na, ho-san - na, ho-

WORDS: Brooke Fraser
MUSIC: Brooke Fraser

HILLSONG HOSANNA
Irr.

[1] san - na in the high - est. ___

[2] san - na in the high - est. ___

Bridge

Heal my heart and make it clean; ___
Break my heart for what breaks yours; ___

o - pen up my eyes to the things un - seen.
ev - ery-thing I am, for your king-dom's cause.

[1] Show me how to love like you ___ have loved me. ___
As I walk from earth in - to ___

[2] ___
___ e - ter - ni - ty. ___

D.S.

___
Ho - san-

⊕ CODA

san - na in the high - est. ___

3189

There Is a Higher Throne

1. There is a high - er throne than all this
2. And there we'll find our home; our life be -

world has known, where faith - ful ones from ev - ery tongue
fore the throne. We'll hon - or him in per - fect song

will one day come. Be - fore the Son we'll stand,
where we be - long. He'll wipe each tear-stained eye

made fault - less through the Lamb; be - liev - ing hearts find
as thirst and hun - ger die. The Lamb be - comes our

prom - ised grace; sal - va - tion comes.
Shep - herd King; we'll reign with him.

Refrain

Hear heav - en's voic - es sing; their thun - derous

an - them rings through em - erald courts and sap - phire skies;

WORDS: Keith Getty and Kristyn Lennox Getty
MUSIC: Keith Getty and Kristyn Lennox Getty

HIGHER THRONE
66.84 D with Refrain

their prais - es rise. All glo - ry, wis - dom, power,

strength, thanks, and hon - or are to God our King, who

reigns on high for - ev - er - more.

3 *Last time*

Mary Had a Little Lamb 3190

1. Ma-ry had a lit - tle Lamb, the ba - by took a
2. Ma-ry saw the Pas - chal Lamb with cross and with a
3. Ma-ry held the Pas - chal Lamb — I am, I was, I
4. Ma-ry saw the Pas - chal Lamb, her own na - ti - vi -
5. Ma-ry, lo, the lit - tle Lamb, the Son is on the

nap; the Sav - ior Christ, the great I Am, lay
crown; the hill - top held the great I Am, all
will — till Ma - ry knew her own I Am and
ty, re - ceived her in - ner Yes I Am, her
throne. The crown is now a di - a - dem and

1-4

sleep - ing on a lap.
hope came tum - bling down.
Ma - ry's heart grew still.
new pros - per - i - ty.

5

we are not a - lone.

WORDS: Herbert Brokering
MUSIC: Jackson Henry

THEOTOKOS
76.86

ACKNOWLEDGMENTS

Use of copyrighted material is gratefully acknowledged by the publisher. Every effort has been made to locate the administrator of each copyright. The publisher would be pleased to have any errors or omissions brought to its attention.

Abingdon Press
(see The Copyright Company)

Sally Ahner
1303 Erin Lane
Nashville TN 37221
Phone: (615) 352-3928

Alfred Music Publishing Co., Inc.
Rights & Permissions
P.O. Box 10003
Van Nuys, CA 91410-0003
permissions@alfred.com

Alletrop Music (see Music Services)

Amity Music
Larry Bonnemere (lbonnemere@wans.net)
OBO the estate of Edward Bonnemere

Ariose Music/Mountain Spring Music
(see EMICMGPublishing.com)

Ateliers et Presses de Taizé
(see GIA Publications, Inc.)

Augsburg Fortress
Attn: Permissions
P.O. Box 1209
Minneapolis MN 55440-1209
Phone: (800) 328-4646

Bridge Building Music
(see Music Services)

Bud John Tunes, Inc.
(see EMICMGPublishing.com)

Carl Fischer, Inc.
65 Bleecker Street
New York, NY 10012
Phone: (212) 777-0900
Fax: (212) 477-6996
All rights assigned to Carl Fischer,
LLC. International copyright secured.
All rights reserved including
performing rights.

Century Oaks Publishing Group/
Richwood Music
(see Conexion Media Group, Inc.)

Susan Palo Cherwien
(see Augsburg Fortress)

Choristers Guild
12404 Park Central Drive
Suite 100
Dallas, TX 75251-1802
(469) 398-3606
(469) 398-3611

Clumsy Fly Music
(see Music Services)

Common Cup Company
276 Chester Court
Coquitlam, BC, Canada V3K 5C3

Conexion Media Group, Inc.
1301 16th Ave. South
Nashville TN 37212
Phone: (615) 250-4600
Fax: (615) 250-4699

Curious? Music UK
(see EMICMGPublishing.com)

Rev. Lisa Ann Moss Degrenia
Community United Methodist Church,
Debary
247 Carmen Lane
DeBary, FL 32713
Phone: (727) 688-2837
Fax: (727) 528-8364

Desert Flower Music
P.O. Box 1476
Carmichael CA 95609
Phone: (916) 481-2999
www.strathdee.com

Delores Duffner
(see OCP Publications)

EMICMGPublishing.com
Apply for license at this web site.
All rights reserved. Used by
permission.

EMICMGPublishing.com
P.O. Box 5084
Brentwood TN 37204-5084
Phone: (615) 371-4400
All rights reserved. Used by
permission.

Isaac Everett
1 St. Nicholas Terrace #23
New York NY 10027
isaac@isaaceverett.com

Kenneth L. Fenton
3100 85th Avenue, North #227
Brooklyn Park, MN 55443
Phone: (763) 657-7069

Fun Attic Music
1710 General George Patton Dr.
Brentwood, TN 37027
(615) 661-4748
pjpub@bellsouth.net

G. Schirmer, Inc.
257 Park Avenue, South
New York NY 10010
Phone: (212) 254-1200
Fax: (212) 254-2013
International copyright secured. All
rights reserved. Used by permission.

Gaither Copyright Management
P.O. Box 737
Alexandria IN 46001
Phone: (765) 724-8233
Fax: (765) 724-8290
Used by permission.

The Rev. F. Richard (Dick) Garland
3 Park Avenue
Derry NH 03038
RevHiker@aol.com

Steve Garnaas-Holmes
271 South Street
Concord NH 03301
stevegarnaasholmes@gmail.com

GIA Publications, Inc.
7404 S. Mason Avenue
Chicago IL 60638
Phone: (800) 442-1358
www.giamusic.com
All rights reserved. Used by
permission.

Carolyn Winfrey Gillette
2606 Salem Drive
Wilmington DE 19808-2198
bcgillette@comcast.net

Gloworks Limited
(see EMICMGPublishing.com)

William P. Gorton
201 W. Hermosa Dr., #B102
Tempe AZ 85282
william@gortonmuse.com

Hal Leonard Corporation
Attn: Copyright Department
7777 West Bluemound Road
P.O. Box 13819
Milwaukee, WI 53213
Fax: (414) 774-3259
hlcopyright@halleonard.com
All rights reserved. International
copyright secured. Used by
permission. Reprinted by permission
of Hal Leonard Corporation.

Dr. Barbara Hamm
P. O. Box 1125
Benicia, CA 94510-4125
mstaize@yahoo.com

Harold Flammer, Inc.
(see Hal Leonard Corporation)

Jackson W. Henry
1267 North Rutherford Blvd.
Murfreesboro, TN 37130
jackson@stmarkstn.org

Bret Hesla
(see Augsburg Fortress)

Hillsong Publishing
(see EMICMGPublishing.com)

Hollis Music, Inc.
c/o The Richmond Organization
266 West 37th Street, 17th Floor
New York NY 1018-6609
Phone: (212) 594-9795
Fax: (212) 594-9782
International copyright secured. Made
in USA. All rights reserved including
public performance for profit. Used by
permission.

Hope Publishing Company
380 South Main Place
Carol Stream IL 60188
Phone: (800) 323-1049
Fax: (630) 665-2552
Apply for license at
www.hopepublishing.com
All rights reserved. Used by
permission

ICEL (International Commission on
English in the Liturgy)
1522 K Street NW
Washingto DC 20005-1202
Phone: (202) 347-0800
Fax: (202) 347-1839

Integrity Music, Inc.
(see EMICMGPublishing.com)

IzzySolSongs
(see Metro One)

Kid Brothers of St. Frank Publishing
(see Music Services)

Kirkland House Music
(see The Lorenz Corporation)

Marienne Kreitlow
Living Song
7616 25th St. SW
Howard Lake, MN 55349
kreitlow@cmgate.com

Doreen Lankshear-Smith
P.O. Box 10155
Thunder Bay Ontario P7B 6T7
doreenls@web.ca

Latter Rain Music
(see EMICMGPublishing.com)

Licensing Associates
935 Broad Street, #31
Bloomfield, NJ 07003
kathleenkarcher@hotmail.com

LifeWay Worship
One LifeWay Plaza
Nashville, TN 37234
All rights reserved. Used by
permission. Apply for license at www.
lifeway.com/PermissionsRequest

Lilly Mack Music
(see EMICMGPublishing.org)

LNWHymns.com
(see Music Services)

Jay D. Locklear
263 Pressly Foushee Road
Sanford, NC 27330
jaylocklear@saintlukeumc.org

Maranatha Praise, Inc.
(see Music Services)

Martin and Morris Studio, Inc.
(see Alfred Music Publishing Co., Inc.)

Raquel Mora Martinez
14710 Kinsem
San Antonio, TX 78248
raqmart2003@yahoo.com

Dean McIntyre
2501 Ravine Dr.
Nashville TN 37217-3614
imdbm@comcast.net

Meaux Mercy
(see EMICMGPublishing.com)

Mercy/Vineyard Publishing
(see Music Services)

Metro One
104 Whitefish Hills Drive
Whitefish, MT 59937
brianray@me.com

Rev. John Middleton
41 Pine Tree Street
Lexington TN 38351
jbmiddleton@bellsouth.net

Music Services
5409 Maryland Way
Suite 200
Brentwood, TN 37027
Apply at musicservices.org for license
All rights reserved. Used by
permission.

New Spring Publishing, Inc./Never
Say Never Songs
(see Music Services)

OCP Publications
Attn: Licensing Department
5536 NE Hassalo
Portland OR 97213-3638
Phone: (503) 281-1191
Fax: (503) 282-3486

Oxford University Press
Great Clarendon Street
Oxford UK OX2 6DP
Reproduced by permission of Oxford
University Press. All rights reserved.

Phil Madeira Music
(See Fun Attic Music)

Pilot Point Music
(see Music Services)

The Pilgrim Press
700 Prospect Avenue
Cleveland OH 44115-1100
Phone: (216) 736-3757

Phil Posthuma
2840 Dell Ridge Drive
Holt, MI 48842
phil.posthuma@trinitywired.com

Praisecharts Publishing
Suite 123
#505-8840 210th St.
Langley, BC V1M 2Y2 Canada
copyright@praisecharts.com

Patrick Roache
(see GIA Publications, Inc.)

Ernest Sands
(see OCP Publications)

Greg Scheer
Church of the Servant
3835 Burton, SE
Grand Rapids, MI 49546
Phone: (616) 956-7611x11

Daniel L. Schutte
(see OCP Publications)

Adam Seate
1605 East Pine Street
Goldsboro, NC 27530
adamseate@nccumc.org

Selah Publishing Co., Inc.
4055 Cloverlea Street
Pittsburg, PA 15227
Phone: (412) 886-1020
Fax: (412) 886-1022
All rights reserved. Used by
permission.

Shepherd's Heart Music, Inc.
(see Praisecharts)

Simpleville Music
P.O. Box 40307
Nashville, TN 37204-0307
licensing@simpleville.net

sixsteps Music
(see EMICMGPublishing.com)

j. snodgrass
509 9th Avenue, West
Hendersonville, NC 28791
Phone: (828) 450-7768

Song Solutions Daybreak
(see Music Services)

Stainer & Bell Ltd.
(see Hope Publishing Company)

Storm Boy Music
(see EMICMGPublishing.com)

Thankyou Music
(see EMICMGPublishing.com)

The Copyright Company
P.O. Box 128139
Nashville TN 37212-8139
Phone: 615-244-9848
Fax: 615-244-9850

The General Board of Discipleship of
The United Methodist Church
1908 Grand Avenue
Nashville TN 37212
Phone: (615) 340-7000

The Jubilate Group
(see Hope Publishing Company)

The Lorenz Corporation
501 East Third Street
Dayton OH 45401-0802
Phone: (937) 228-6118
Fax: (937) 223-2042

The United Methodist Publishing House
(see The Copyright Company)

Rev. John D. Thornburg
9553 Atherton Drive
Dallas TX 75243
ethornbu@aol.com

Marilyn E. Thornton
4381 Enchanted Circle
Nashville TN 37218

Josh Tinley
2406 Keeling Drive
Mt. Juliet TN 37122
jtinley@umpublishing.org

Universal Music - MGB Songs
Admin. by Brentwood-Benson Music
Publishing, Inc.
(see Music Services)

Utryck
(see Licensing Associates)

Vamos Publishing
(see EMICMGPublishing.com)

Van Ness Press, Inc.
(see LifeWay Worship)

Vineyard Songs
(see Music Services)

Walton Music Corporation
(see Licensing Associates)

Wayne Leupold Editions, Inc.
8510 Triad Drive
Colfax NC 27235
Phone: (800) 765-3196
wleupold@msn.com

WGRG (Wild Goose Resource Group)
(see GIA Publications, Inc.)

William J. Gaither, Inc.
(see Gaither Copyright Management)

Word Music, LLC
(see Word Music Group, LLC)

Word Music Group, LLC
20 Music Square East
Nashville, TN 37203

Wordspring Music and Songs From
The Indigo Room
(see Word Music Group, LLC)

worshiptogether.com Songs
(see EMICMGPublishing.com)

INDEX OF FIRST LINES AND COMMON TITLES